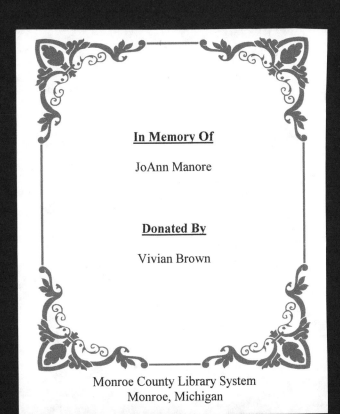

Historic Monuments of
AMERICA

Donald Young

NEW LINE BOOKS

Fax: (888) 719-7723
e-mail: info@newlinebooks.com

Printed and bound in Singapore

ISBN 1-59764-124-3

Visit us on the web!
www.newlinebooks.com

Author: Donald Young
Producer: Robert M. Tod
Designer and Art Director: Mark Weinberg
Editor: Michael Vickerman
Picture Research: Ede Rothaus and Grace How
Associate Art Director: Louise Sullivan

TABLE OF CONTENTS

Mesa Verde National Park, 1929. The Antiquities Act (1906) was a milestone in the movement to protect national resources. It permitted the president to establish national monuments on Federal land, and made it a crime to remove antiquities from the public lands.

Introduction

December 1888. Southwestern Colorado. The two cowboys feel the sting of the wind and the snow against their faces. Their horses step carefully on the thin soil and slippery bare rock of the high mesa. The men, who have not been this way before, are searching for lost cows, but they are about to find a lot more.

They pause at the edge of a deep canyon. A few more steps forward, and they would plunge hundreds of feet into the narrow gorge. As the men look across the canyon to the opposite wall, the swirling snow calms down for a moment, and they can make out a large alcove, several hundred feet long, high on the face of the rock. Within the alcove they discover a lost city, totally empty, completely silent.

The alcove contains hundreds of rooms made of stone. The towers rise four stories, almost touching its roof. Archaeologists will be able to learn that the people who lived in the alcove abandoned it 600 years earlier. No one knows why, for sure. They left tools, jewelry, and pots full of corn behind them. The two cowboys are the first white men ever to see the silent city of stone.

More than a century has passed since Richard Wetherill and his brother-in-law, Charlie Mason, discovered what is now called the Cliff Palace. Now, as then, the high flat plateau is known by its Spanish name, Mesa Verde, meaning "green table." Explorers had found other large cliff dwellings nearby, and Mesa Verde National Park was created in 1906. Today, visitors scramble up and down ladders to enter the large alcoves and gaze in amazement at the buildings the ancient people constructed on the face of the rock walls.

Mesa Verde is unique among the nation's 50 national parks. It is the only one that has been established primarily for its cultural, rather than natural, resources. However, the National Park System encompasses more than 350 units, and more than half of them preserve historical and cultural resources. This book offers a selective look at America's past through a review of the places associated with its history and prehistory that Congress and the president have set aside for Federal protection. A companion volume to this one, *The Natural Monuments of America*, is an introduction to the magnificent mountains,

Many Park System units protect ancient ruins. Because dry climatic conditions in the Southwest have slowed the deterioration of long-abandoned structures, the United States has an unusually rich heritage from its past. This is Chaco Canyon, New Mexico, 1929.

deserts, lakeshores, and seashores of the United States.

What exactly is a monument? The question has more than one answer. Many Park Service monuments meet the dictionary definition of a monument as a memorial stone or a building erected in remembrance of a person or event.

But the word has been given another meaning. The term "national monument" entered the language in 1906 with the signing into law of the Antiquities Act. Until then preservation at the Federal level of government had focused on scenic areas. Yellowstone had been the first national park, in 1872. Three parks in the Sierra Nevada of California, including Yosemite, were added in 1890. Mount Rainier in Washington and Crater Lake in Oregon joined the list around the turn of the century.

Approval of the Antiquities Act grew out of concern for the protection of pre-Columbian ruins in the Southwest. Ransackers had toppled walls with blasting powder at the Cliff Palace, and were using thousand-year-old beams for firewood. The Antiquities Act, signed by President Theodore Roosevelt, prohibited the removal of any historic object from the public lands. Furthermore, the president could, on his own authority and without the approval of Congress, establish "national monuments" from lands within the public domain.

Roosevelt, in the three remaining years of his presidency, created 18 national monuments. Today about 80 units within the Park System bear that designation. But the definition is not yet precise. The status of "national monument" has been imposed on Anasazi ruins, battlefields, forts, glaciers, caves, and the birthplaces of the famous.

In the same year the Antiquities Act became law, Mesa Verde was proclaimed a national park by Congress. Ten years later, in 1916, Congress approved creation of the National Park Service to oversee the administration of the parks and monuments, which by then numbered 35 in all.

By the time Horace Albright became director of the

National Park Service in 1929 there were 54 parks and monuments, and Albright had identified a new mission for the Service that would double the number of its units. Civil War veterans had faithfully preserved the sites of the battles in which they had participated, and oversight supervision of these now-quiet, gravestone-studded landscapes had, for the most part, become the responsibility of the War Department.

Many of those in the Park Service, accustomed to attending to the welfare of herds of elk and buffalo, were not ready, by inclination or training, to take on the preservation of historical monuments. But Albright wanted the battlefields in the Park System and he was supported by others in the Park Service who regarded conservation of history to be a plausible extension of the idea of conserving nature.

With the approach of the bicentennial of the birth of the "Father of Our Country," Congress approved in 1930 the establishment of the George Washington Birthplace National Monument within the Park System. Funds were provided for the reconstruction of his birthplace, and history had a foot in the Park Service door. In the same year Colonial National Monument was established which included Jamestown Island, the first permanent English settlement in the future United States, and Yorktown, where Washington's army won the decisive victory over the British during the Revolution.

Finally, in 1933, by executive order, President Franklin Roosevelt transferred nearly 50 historical sites—battlefields, cemeteries, and military parks—from other agencies to the Park Service. Many more historical units have been added since then.

While most of the history units are not officially "monuments," they certainly are within the purview of this book. It should be noted, furthermore, that as a result of the efforts of veterans' and patriotic organizations, the Civil War battlefields in particular are dotted with tons of granite and marble statuary that meet the dictionary definition of monument. By the way, the monuments of war heroes usually adhere to this convention: if his steed has one hoof in the air, the subject on horseback was wounded in the battle. Two hooves in the air, and the rider was slain in combat.

The definition of monument, then, will be left sufficiently flexible to include even the ruts of the Sante Fe Trail, still visible within Fort Union National Monument—ruts that are monuments to human progress!

The units of the Park System have been sorted out—with appreciation for subtleties that most of us might overlook—into 23 classifications. In addition to parks, monuments, and historic sites, there are national memorials, parkways, preserves, recreation areas, scenic trails, historical parks, a historical preserve, a mall, and so forth. There are national military parks, battlefields, battlefield parks, and one battlefield site.

But what does all this mass of acreage say about America's past and it people?

For one thing, the Park System pays homage to the ethnic diversity of the citizens of the United States. Sixteenth and 17th century settlements along the East Coast by the English, Spanish, and the French, barely more visible in the light of history than in the mists of legend, have been reconstructed or restored according to fragments of information culled from layers of soil and yellowed documents. Touro Synagogue National Historic Site recalls the early Jewish experience in Colonial America that textbooks may ignore. Ellis Island, in New York Harbor, memorializes people who were of many nationalities before they became hyphenated Americans, and then just Americans.

And the Park System offers ample reminders that before Americans were English, Spanish, Irish, and Vietnamese, they were cave dwellers and cliff dwellers, mound builders and painters of pictographs. Americans were also missionaries, ranchers, poets, and slaves. They were criminals, prisoners of war, lepers, and drowning victims.

The humble beginnings and often equally humble lives of Americans are a distinguishing feature of the past as revealed in the historic sites. While Europe beckons the visitor with its many castle/birthplaces of men born to rule, the National Park System offers instead the preserved, restored, or reconstructed log cabins of great Americans. Those born in these cabins had a lot in common, too—the will to succeed, and the knowledge that in America it was possible to do so.

Blacks who graduated from log cabins included Booker T. Washington, born a slave in Virginia, and George Washington Carver, the son of an unknown father in Missouri.

The landscapes of war are not interpreted merely in terms of strategic maneuvers by West Point graduates. National Park Service historians recreate, as well, the stories of humble common soldiers, resisting death from freezing at Valley Forge or fighting boredom under the endless sky above a frontier fort.

And of course the story of prehistoric Americans, and of those who met the white man's ships, is that of humble peoples clinging to religious ritual and a determination to survive, scratching out a sustenance from often hostile soil or hunting wild animals on nearly even terms, without a written language, with little reason to expect that life would ever get any better, innocent of any concept of human progress.

Next, what can be said about America's violent past? Dozens of monuments within the Park System are mileposts in the history of human strife. On the other hand, none of America's idyllic "Our Towns" has been preserved in amber, or otherwise, as part of the Park System. They just don't have, in the bureaucrat's terminology, a "nationally significant resource." Therefore, quaint New England villages won't be subjected to guided tours every day at 2 p.m. by men and women wearing green hats.

(You may step back into the past at one of many community-wide historic restorations supported by private associations or corporations, sometimes assisted by government money. Williamsburg, Virginia, the grandest historical restoration in the country, is linked by the Colonial Parkway to NPS sites in Jamestown and Yorktown, but Williamsburg itself is privately owned.)

In truth, then, those so-called nationally significant resources (aside from the prehistoric sites) generally recall Americans at times of conflict.

The American Revolution and the Civil War were by far the two most traumatic experiences on domestic soil, and historians still argue about whether they could have been avoided. And what about the other wars? The preponderance of evidence is that America could never have been won by those unwilling to fight over it, and even most of those who fought—the Spanish, British, Mexicans, Apaches, Sioux—did not prevail.

Someone once complained that someday the only green places left in the East would be battlefields and golf courses. The commitment to create more parks and other natural areas, state and national, will avert that circumstance to some degree. In any event, visitors often are struck by the ironic calm of a former killing field, tucked away within the whir of 20th century life.

Also in the "small consolation" category, violence and conflict have always given rise to the most heartfelt and emotional expressions of art. The Lincoln and Vietnam Veterans memorials are particularly moving remembrances of an assassinated president and 58,000 casualties of war.

However, to see the national historical monuments as a chronology of revolution, war, and other conflict is to miss the point somewhat. The true essence of the most notable Americans, those who became a part of history, may not be apparent from that perspective. Their common denominator will be found elsewhere, more closely associated with what they were than what they did.

Few nations, if any, have put up so many monuments to dreamers and idealists. For example, one must marvel, really, at the remarkable concentration of great minds produced in time to pull off the American Revolution. One can logically conclude that, indeed, just enough time had elapsed from the arrival of the Pilgrims in 1620 to the Boston Massacre in 1770—a century and a half—for colonial Americans to clear the land, build their homes, sink roots and create means of livelihood, establish institutions of local government, and develop communications with other colonies.

These communications led, in turn, to the emergence of a large number of great writers, orators, and, yes, agitators. In short, the Revolution probably could not have happened 50 years earlier, and it probably could not have been avoided for another 50 years, even with greater gestures of conciliation on the part of King and Parliament. But what really made it succeed was some impulse embedded in the psyche, or soul, of those who chose to take their chances in the New World, and it was this same impulse, or drive, that propelled their descendants toward the goal of establishing a representative government that would protect the natural rights of its citizens. It is easy now to forget just how radical were the views of Thomas Jefferson and Thomas Paine for their times. It cannot be mere coincidence that their beliefs and those of their comrades found full flower in a particular land at a particular time.

Other wars, too, were fought over ideas. America has had no War of the Roses, with armies clashing with the sole object of putting one prince or another on the throne. The Civil War was fought on one side over the essential need to preserve the Union and to free the slaves, and on the other side over the right of a society to perpetuate an economic and social system that the society genuinely believed worked to the benefit of all and would continue to work if only the national government would not interfere.

(World War I was a war America might have skipped while waiting for the big one. But a president driven by ideals—insuring freedom of the seas, making the world safe for democracy—guided the people toward war and prepared them to accept it.)

And thus, so many of the historical monuments of the Revolutionary era and the Civil War are to individuals with ideas—Jefferson, Washington, Lincoln. The likenesses of those three appear on Mount Rushmore, along with a portrait of Theodore Roosevelt, a visionary who

was forever hacking away at the Gordian knots in other people's minds. "Is there any law that will prevent me from declaring Pelican Island a Federal Bird Reservation?", he once asked. "Very well, then I so declare it!"

There were many other ideas whose time would come in America, and national monuments honor some of those who first espoused them. For example, Elizabeth Cady Stanton, who was tired of caring for children and doing other "women's work" while her husband traveled freely, organized the first Women's Rights Convention.

Rosa Parks was tired, too, tired of having to stand in the back of a bus. No Park Service site is named after her, but by taking a seat up front in the white section she helped trigger the Montgomery, Alabama, bus boycott that brought someone who is so honored, the Rev. Martin Luther King, Jr., to national prominence. "I have a dream," King said in his greatest address, "that my four little children will one day live in a nation where they will not be judged by the color of their skin but by the content of their character." Jefferson survived the revolution he helped launch with the penning of the Declaration of Independence, but King's dream would require even more effort and time to realize, and his unflagging commitment to that vision cost him his life.

National historic sites and monuments recall failed dreams, too. John Brown, crossing the boundary between idealist and fanatic, could not induce slaves to join an

A scene at Manassas, Virginia, during the Civil War. For the past century, except for Pearl Harbor, the United States has been spared the scourge of war on its own soil. But the Park System contains many sites dating from the American Revolution, the Civil War, and the Indian conflicts.

Harpers Ferry, West Virginia, following some of the devastation it experienced during the Civil War. Many historic buildings have been restored. Historic preservation and restoration are major concerns of the Park Service.

armed revolt against their masters. The 24 scattered sites of Nez Percé National Monument in Idaho are suggestive of the shattered dream of Chief Joseph, who had fought to keep the homeland of his people in the face of the white man's advance. Ruined 17th century missions in the Southwest recall the largely unsuccessful efforts by Spanish priests to convert Native Americans to Christianity.

America was a nation filled with dreamers, not all possessed with the rhetorical gifts of a Jefferson or a Dr. King, but they knew well what they wanted, and their principal goals were encapsulated in the phrases *American Dream* and *Manifest Destiny*.

American Dream appears not to have entered the language until the 20th century, though the idea is older. At its simplest, this Dream meant a home of one's own, however humble, one which the highest leader of the nation—even a king, if there were one—would not enter without permission.

Beyond that, the Dream is an American social ideal that stresses egalitarianism and, especially, material prosperity. The Second Continental Congress gave its blessing to the former in adopting Jefferson's Declaration with the line "all men are created equal…" And in his reference to "Life, Liberty and the pursuit of Happiness" the last word can be read as a green light to pursue the good life.

In 1845, following the annexation of Texas by the United States, a magazine article proclaimed "our manifest destiny to overspread the continent allotted by Providence for the free development of our multiplying millions." This catch phrase, implying divine sanction for

U.S. territorial expansion, was used by advocates of the annexation of Mexican territory after the Mexican War and of the Oregon country disputed with Great Britain. The purchase of Alaska was welcomed by the exponents of Manifest Destiny, who also focused their eyes beyond the shores, to Hawaii, Guam, and even the Philippines.

The nation today represents the fulfillment, to the extent that proved possible, of the American Dream and Manifest Destiny. The United States did span the continent, and added a few islands at sea as well. In a land of private homes, most of the people can indeed point to their small piece of the American Dream.

The Dream and the Destiny are not overlooked in the National Park System. Homestead National Monument in Nebraska honors the act of Congress that awarded free land to pioneers. Forts on the Great Plains mark the 19th century boundaries of a frontier that was pushed ever westward until it disappeared. Western battlefield sites are painful reminders that white men's dreams could not accommodate the survival of the way of life that Native Americans had known.

At one time most Americans also imagined that they had divine support for clearing and subduing the wilderness. The natural units of the Park System, from Everglades National Park in Florida to Gates of the Arctic National Park and Preserve in Alaska, constitute areas that somehow survived the onslaught, although some of them still remain threatened by human activity of one sort or another. Nevertheless, their inclusion in the Park System represents a sea change in American attitudes toward the real world.

Ultimately, what the forts, gravestones, log cabins, and cliff dwellings of the National Park System say about America's past and its people depends on the individual visitor. Meaning, like beauty, is in the eye of the beholder. The parks don't tell the whole story; too much has been lost to the wear and tear of time and to calculated or unintentional destruction. A visitor fortified with a history course or two and an inquiring mind can step back into America's past and begin to appreciate why events unfolded as they did, and perhaps even surmise how everything might have come out differently.

September. A national battlefield in the pleasant rolling country not far from Washington, D. C. The stalks in the cornfield in front of you stand stiff and dry, just skeletons of plants. Back in the 1860s, on the day of the battle, the cannon fire was so intense that the stalks were leveled to the ground. The woods to your left were set ablaze as Rebel and Union soldiers ran among the trees, firing their rifles. The flames consumed the helpless wounded.

On your right, a straight narrow road runs past the cornfield and disappears over the crest of a low hill. On the morning of the battle men had marched down the road shoulder to shoulder, confident of victory, eager to fight. Late that afternoon, billowing dust off the road almost obscured the setting sun and the horse-drawn wagons that moved back up the road. The wagons were loaded with wounded soldiers, some crying, some unconscious, some missing an arm or a leg.

You look across the road. The buildings of a shopping mall run along the road for hundreds of feet. A flashing sign, rising above the buildings, announces a special sale on back-to-school clothes. Music from a loudspeaker promotes a store selling records and tapes. The brakes of automobiles squeal as the vehicles maneuver in the crowded parking lot.

You feel cheated. The solemn mood of the battlefield and the adjacent graveyard is shattered. You had come to this place to try to understand why men had sacrificed their lives for something that they believed in. In the words of Abraham Lincoln, this land is hallowed ground. But the owners of the shopping mall don't believe that. And the members of Congress, who fill their speeches with tributes to the heroes of American history, wouldn't spend the money to buy the land to keep the battlefield the way it was on the day thousands died.

Today, the national parks, monuments, and historic sites face many threats. As suggested by the composite example given above, battlefields in Maryland and Virginia have been or may be overrun as the suburbs push farther out from the cities. Usually, not enough land was set aside or purchased to preserve the original scene.

The developer of one shopping center planned to turn the headquarters of General Robert E. Lee at Manassas (Bull Run) into a parking lot. Shops were to be built on the site of the field hospital. Almost too late, Congress in

1988 approved a bill to buy the property adjacent to the battlefield where the South won two victories. Without the law, almost certainly the remains of soldiers lying in unmarked graves near the site of a hospital would have been paved over. But saying no to suburban sprawl carried a high price tag in this case. This law, which includes a plan to eliminate two highways cutting through the battlefield and relocating them elsewhere, set taxpayers back $60 million. Had Congress given the battlefield full protection from the outset, before roads were built and land values soared, the cost would have been far less.

Antietam National Battlefield, farther than Manassas from Washington's ever-spreading suburbs, faced an even more parlous situation before Congress acted a second time in 1988. The Park Service owned only 815 acres within the 3,200-acre boundary of the battlefield. About half of the remainder was under scenic easements that restricted development. But the Miller cornfield, which still looks as it did on September 17, 1862 when it saw the fiercest fighting in the bloodiest day in American history (23,000 casualties), was in private hands and unprotected even by an easement. The 1988 law lifted the limit on the number of acres the Park Service can buy within the park boundary.

Antietam's setting is pastoral and now, perhaps, it will remain that way, serene, empty even of visitors in the chill pale gauzy dawns that evoke the morning when the carnage transformed the cornfield into a mass morgue. If no battle had been fought at Antietam the landscape would be worth preserving just for its charming 19th century rusticity. But Antietam's beauty can be painful if one stands where a photographer stood after the battle, and looks at his portraits, heaps of death.

The "battles" to save Antietam and Manassas may have been won, at least temporarily, but Fredericksburg, in Virginia, is hopelessly overrun. The slopes above the Rappahannock River that the Confederates defended against the advancing Federals are filled with the artifacts of modernity. In any attempt to re-enact this battle on the original site today, the impact of shells would turn self-service pumps into infernos and adorn backyards and patios with barbecue pits their upscale owners hadn't planned on.

It is not enough to be able to read in a book about a great event or a tragic chapter in American history. The place where it happened must be protected. The columnist George Will has written that the failure to preserve an historic site has serious consequences: the loss of history itself and our ability to remember it.

Historic preservation and restoration is a major challenge to the Park Service, especially considering that there is never enough money available in the budget. As noted, more than half of the Park System units are managed primarily for their historical or cultural resources, and many of the natural areas also contain important historic buildings and relics of prehistoric peoples. Historic structures within the parks, battlefields, and other units number more than 10,000, and the Service estimates that it has more than 10 million "museum objects and artifacts of historic significance."

Although the sites selected are not in the Park System, the Park Service since the 1930s has undertaken the National Survey of Historic Sites and Buildings and has identified more than 1,000 buildings that have been designated as National Historic Landmarks. Owners usually agree to cooperate in preserving the site, and a bronze plaque is placed on the building identifying its role in American history. The contribution of the Park Service in protecting and restoring historic buildings has been immense.

Left alone, nature will heal its own wounds. Someday, Yellowstone will closely resemble its appearance before the devastating fires in the summer of 1988. However, sad to say, natural processes are not the servants of history. Trees will grow again in Yellowstone, but any 19th century cabin or other noteworthy wooden structure caught up in the conflagration vanished forever. Elsewhere, waves assault shorelines, destroy the beaches, and threaten to topple buildings. Indeed, one East Coast lighthouse may soon collapse into the sea. Tornadoes, earthquakes, and severe fluctuations in temperatures take their toll. Much of history is on paper, and improper storage allows humidity to yellow, curl, and dissolve the documents.

In its report *National Parks for a New Generation*

The national cemetery at Vicksburg, Mississippi. Caring for the remains of thousands of men and women who fought in wars is a major responsibility of the National Park Service.

(1985), the Conservation Foundation concluded that the Park Service's highest priority was the natural areas, and that its central mission is associated with scenery, not battlefields, "with Old Faithful, not the Liberty Bell." The foundation asserted that in units bearing a "natural" designation any settlements, ranches, foundries, or other buildings were treated as intrusions on the natural scene, and potential candidates for razing. One official was quoted as saying he wanted "to get rid of old buildings" in his park whenever possible. One person's historic building is someone else's meaningless eyesore. The decisions on what to keep are not always easy ones.

In 1859 a geologist, John Newberry, discovered a large abandoned ruin in northern New Mexico. It was in a fair state of preservation, its walls 25 feet high in places. But in 1878, just 19 years later, the anthropologist Lewis Morgan found that a fourth of the pueblo's stones had been hauled away by settlers for use as building material.

A few years after that, local youths discovered something the more experienced explorers had overlooked. Breaking through a wall, they found a room with 13 burials and a large trove of Anasazi artifacts, including pots, baskets, feather cloaks, and beads and ornaments. Word soon spread, and within a short time these important clues to life in the United States a thousand years ago had disappeared. This site, Aztec Ruins National Monument, now enjoys Federal protection.

But the looting goes on elsewhere. Investigating this loss of the nation's heritage for *National Parks* magazine, Jim Robbins found increasing demand by collectors for a variety of ancient relics. The decision in 1971 by Sotheby Parke Bernet Galleries to auction pre-Columbian artifacts sharply stimulated interest in the market overnight. One basket sold for $152,000. Those of ordinary design or workmanship go for $10,000. An unbroken mug will bring in $200. Collecting on a budget? You can pick up a human skull for $50.

With thousands of sites to guard on the public lands, employees of the National Park Service, the National Forest Service, and the Bureau of Land Management are simply outmanned. In Alaska, where the Park Service has one officer for every four million acres, catching looters is largely a matter of chance.

The Antiquities Act of 1906 did not prohibit collecting on private land. In the West, a large portion of the total acreage is in the public domain, and its complete protection is impossible. In any event, digging for pots and whatever has always been a popular pastime for individuals and families in the West, without much concern about who owns the land.

What is new is the level of sophistication of the diggers. Use of metal detectors on battlefields to turn up shell fragments and other scraps of war is bad enough. The recent use of bulldozers—not a vehicle of choice for professional archaeologists—to assault ancient ruins introduces a level of destruction heretofore unknown. When the pothunters are finished with a site, whatever is left and the layers of soil are so churned up that the professionals are unable to interpret their meaning.

Archaeologists and the museums and universities they serve have not been free of criticism either. Tons of artifacts have been removed from the major sites, and the vast majority of it is stashed in vaults, seldom exhibited, and out of human sight except to a bare handful of researchers. Ironically, a looted pot, displayed in a collector's home, will be seen over time by a greater number of people.

Many Native Americans make no distinction between archaeologists and looters. They have protested strongly against what they see as desecration of their ancestors' burial grounds and removal of human remains and other objects. Universities and museums are coming under pressure to return some of their accumulations and to rebury bones.

The National Park System grew rapidly in the decades before 1980. In that year the passage of the Alaska National Interest Lands Conservation Act resulted in a doubling of the acreage of the Park System. A few small natural parks and monuments have been added since, and others are under consideration. But it is apparent

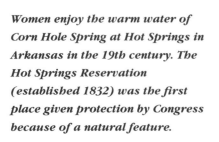

Women enjoy the warm water of Corn Hole Spring at Hot Springs in Arkansas in the 19th century. The Hot Springs Reservation (established 1832) was the first place given protection by Congress because of a natural feature.

that almost all of the major remaining natural landscapes and ecosystems are already in the system or in wildlife preserves or under state protection.

Historical units are added from time to time, and few of those "nationally significant resources" are still outside the system and available for acquisition. States and localities have protected a few themselves, and so have private organizations. Williamsburg, Monticello, and Mount Vernon are in these categories of protection, as are the Alamo and Bodie, perhaps the West's best-preserved ghost town. Whatever the ownership, the important thing is that America has access to a great deal of its past.

Some important non-National Park System sites are included in this book, to help round out the historical overview. On the other hand, space limitations herein do not permit a discussion or illustration of every historical and cultural unit in the system.

Park Service personnel are defensive about maintaining the quality of the system, and some complaints have been raised that too many units have been added. The Conservation Foundation noted in its report that some recent additions are "undeniably obscure," and added that Allegheny Portage Railway and Maggie Walker National Historic Site "are not on anyone's list of world-class wonders."

Another controversy relates to the reconstruction or restoration of buildings. Purists argue that ruins should be left untouched, so that whatever is there can be seen as it was found, with no introduction of human guesswork as to how the building would have appeared. For historic buildings that have disappeared, reconstruction can be based on existing drawings or photographs. Sometimes an old fort has been constructed based on only the faintest evidence of foundations.

At Saugus Iron Works National Historic Site in Massachusetts, only the Iron Works House is original. The furnace, blacksmith shop, forge, mill, and ironhouse were built in the 1950s by the American Iron and Steel Institute to illustrate the iron industry of the 17th century. The new buildings may not be of the past, but they represent a good-faith effort to enlighten us about a time that is very nearly beyond retrieval.

Park Service actors dressed in period costumes and serving as hostesses or demonstrating crafts are not common in the System, and this feature is more likely to be found in private restorations.

Today, the past exists rather uneasily with the present and with the prospect of future growth. In cities, 18th century brick or wood structures are often snuggled in among modern skyscrapers, still somehow displaying more class and a sense of belonging than the glass-sheathed behemoths that cast shadows upon them. Boston, more innovative than some cities, is putting its old buildings to modern community and commercial uses, and on the skyline of the 1990s the Old North Church steeple and the Customs House clock tower hold their own alongside the new.

Some other historic sites are very much a part of the present, too. Services are conducted at Touro Synagogue in Rhode Island. Ford's Theatre, where Lincoln was shot, is an active, legitimate theatre, putting on a full schedule of plays each year.

Why do we want to preserve the past and to relive it in visits to historic sites? Some people think that life in some other era was easier, simpler, less of a hassle. But pain and stress and struggle were endemic to the lives of most Americans—homesteaders, soldiers, slaves, immigrants in squalid city tenements. This is made clear in the honest interpretations of centuries gone by that are presented by Park Service personnel for visitors. We appreciate that truth, and most of us, after a few days trudging across a battlefield or peering at squiggles carved into a canyon wall, are content to return to a world of green-lettered screens and taped movies.

Nonetheless, we cannot escape history. As we grow older we will find that we have traveled through more of it, and experienced more of it, even if only vicariously on the television news. The impulse grows to extend our time line backward as well as forward, to identify the footpaths of the past and follow them to the present, as a means of trying to determine where they will lead next.

THE NORTHEAST

The obelisk atop Breed's Hill north of Boston marks the site of the first major battle in the war for American Independence—called, inaccurately, the Battle of Bunker Hill. The Americans retreated after inflicting substantial losses on the British, who subsequently evacuated Boston.

The fighting in the American Revolution began on April 19, 1775, when 3,500 militiamen, called minutemen, fought 1,700 British regulars on a stretch of country road west of Boston. The Minute Man Statue stands at Concord, where the colonists first stood their ground and fought.

16

BY THE RUDE BRIDGE THAT
ARCHED THE FLOOD,
THEIR FLAG TO APRIL'S
BREEZE UNFURLED;
HERE ONCE THE EMBATTLED
FARMERS STOOD
AND FIRED THE SHOT HEARD
ROUND THE WORLD.

In Boston's Faneuil Hall, the "Cradle of Liberty," Samuel Adams and James Otis spoke out against the oppressive taxes imposed by Great Britain. A meeting that began here on December 16, 1773, to protest the tax on tea led later that night to the dumping of tea in the harbor—the Boston Tea Party.

On April 18, 1775, Paul Revere and William Dawes rode from Boston to warn Colonial leaders that armed British troops were on the way. The church sexton hung two lanterns in the steeple of the Old North Church to signal that the British were coming by sea, not by land.

A spirit of independence, an impulse toward freedom, burns within each of us. But if effective resistance to an oppressive government is to be made, then united action must be taken. Beliefs and ideals must be articulated, and a plan devised for throwing off the yoke of unwanted, unrepresentative authority. In the city of Boston historic buildings where patriots first gathered to decry the heavy-handed rule of King George III and Parliament still stand. They are among the structures included in Boston National Historical Park.

The Old State House (1713), a squat brick building at the head of State Street, was the seat of colonial government, and in 1766 a gallery was opened to permit the public to watch its government in action. It was here that James Otis argued that Parliament could not take from the colonists certain fundamental rights, including the right to have their homes and property secure against search or seizure. And it was on the cobbled street outside the Old State House on the evening of March 5, 1770 that a confrontation with British soldiers, fought on the American side with snowballs, ended with the shooting deaths of five protestors—the Boston Massacre.

Not far away, Faneuil Hall became a place of assembly for many protests against British actions, including imposition of the Stamp Act, and its second floor, above a market, contained the meeting

The clash at North Bridge over the Concord River was just a skirmish, and many Americans were still reluctant to break away from the motherland. The Declaration of Independence was not adopted until more than a year had passed.

The Charlestown Navy Yard, across the Charles River from downtown Boston, is the home of the USS Constitution, which was launched in 1797. The world's oldest commissioned warship, "Old Ironsides" sailed against the Barbary pirates and fought the British in the War of 1812. It never lost a battle.

hall that Otis called the Cradle of Liberty. Crowds too large to fit into Faneuil Hall would move to the Old South Meeting House, built in 1729 as a Congregational Church. After protesting a new British tax on tea on December 16, 1773, citizens disguised as Indians left Old South, headed for the waterfront, boarded three ships, and dumped their cargoes into the bay, adding the name Boston Tea Party to the cavalcade of history.

Boston's oldest surviving house (1680) was the home of Paul Revere from 1770 to 1800. Here he achieved lasting renown as a silversmith and produced his famous engraving of the Boston Massacre. He lived here in the fateful spring of 1775, and on April 18 he rode west toward Lexington to warn John Hancock and Samuel Adams that the British were coming to arrest them. From the steeple of Old North Church, sexton Robert Newman hung two lanterns to alert Charlestown that the British were coming by sea, not by land.

William Dawes also rode with the news, and 77 armed militiamen were waiting for 700 British troops at Lexington Common. A brief exchange of fire in which eight patriots were killed inaugurated the military phase of the resistance. At Concord, five miles further west, where the British sought to confiscate arms stashed by the colonials, the militiamen stood as an organized fighting unit against the British and "by the rude bridge that arched the flood" they "fired the shot heard round the world," in Emerson's phrase. This clash took place at the North Bridge, over the Concord River. Named for the fallen militiamen who were prepared to fight on a minute's notice, the Minute Man Statue marks their stand on the west side of the reconstructed bridge.

Two months later, the British planned to occupy Charlestown Heights, north of Boston across the Charles River. The colonials fortified Breed's Hill, prompting a British attack on June 17. The

General Washington used this house as his headquarters during the siege of Boston in 1776. Early in the 19th century the owner took in lodgers, one of whom was Henry Wadsworth Longfellow. Later, Longfellow's father-in-law purchased the house as a wedding present for his daughter and Longfellow.

Americans fell back after inflicting heavy losses on the British, and the (misnamed) Bunker Hill Monument marks the site of the Revolution's first major engagement.

Cambridge, across the Charles River to the west of Boston and accessible to it on the Longfellow Bridge, is the location of Longfellow National Historic Site. The Longfellow home (1759) served as George Washington's headquarters during the siege of Boston, and here in 1776 he and Martha celebrated their 17th wedding anniversary. The poet Henry Wadsworth Longfellow, who first stayed at the house as a lodger, lived there for 45 years until his death in 1882.

In Quincy, just south of Boston, stands the "Old House" in which four generations of the Adams family, including two presidents, lived between 1788 and 1927. Built soon after 1730, and expanded and redesigned several times by the Adamses, the house is an architectural curiosity, but its furnishings are original and its library alone is a capsule of 150 years of American political and literary history.

A future president, John F. Kennedy, was born at 83 Beals Street in the Boston suburb of Brookline in 1917. He and his family moved elsewhere in the neighborhood when he was four years old, but after his death the Kennedy family repurchased the house. His mother supervised the restoration, returning many original pieces of furniture.

John Fitzgerald Kennedy, the 35th president of the United States, was born in the master bedroom of this frame house in the Boston suburb of Brookline on a warm spring day in 1917. He lived here with his family until he was four years old, when they moved to a larger house a few blocks away.

Yankee enterprise is remembered at Salem Maritime National Historic Site, 15 miles northeast of Boston. In the 1640s, within two decades of the landing of the Pilgrims, Salem's ships—single-deck sloops and schooners—were carrying cod and lumber to the West Indies in exchange for molasses and rum. During the Revolution, many of the ships were licensed privateers that harassed British ports and commandeered munitions and supplies for the American army. For three decades after independence was won, Salem was a shipping center of world importance, opening to U.S. trade such exotic ports as Calcutta, Manila, Kronstadt (St. Petersburg), Zanzibar, Madras, and Mombassa. A few wharves survive, and buildings include the home of Elias Hasket Derby, probably America's first millionaire.

The entrepreneurial spirit is also recalled 28 miles northwest of Boston in "the city of spindles." This city, Lowell, was named for Francis Cabot Lowell, a Boston merchant who visited English textile factories in 1811 and was impressed with their advanced technology. Back in the United States, Lowell oversaw development of an advanced power loom that made possible the transformation of cotton into finished cloth within a single factory. Lowell and other investors established the Merrimack Manufacturing Company between the Pawtucket Canal and the Merrimack and Concord rivers in a small village.

Within a few years more mills were constructed, utilizing the power of the falls to run the machinery. Chelmsford (later named Lowell) boomed, becoming one of the world's leading textile centers. Young female immigrants from many nations found steady, if low-paid, employment in the mills. The industry has long since declined, but its heyday is captured in the well-preserved structures of Lowell National Historical Park.

New York, another state steeped in history, contains many sites within the National Park System. Fort Stanwix, in Rome, is a faithful reconstruction of a fort that figured prominently in the American Revolution. The British built Fort Stanwix in 1758 on a strategic spot between the Mohawk River

The Custom House (left) and other houses at Salem Maritime National Historic Site recall the early 19th century days when Salem, Massachusetts was one of the world's great trading centers. Its ships sailed around the Cape of Good Hope to the Far East and India, and to other exotic ports.

The Lowell Mill Girl Statue at Lowell National Historical Park honors the young New England farm women who toiled for 12 hours a day, six days a week in the 19th century and by their labors helped make Lowell, Massachussetts one of the country's major textile centers.

The Worker statue in Lowell, Massachusetts. This was America's first planned industrial city, and at one time its eight mills employed 7,500 people. Dangerous and exhausting working conditions encouraged the growth of the labor movement and led to eventual employee affiliation with the Industrial Workers of the World.

23

and Wood Creek. Later abandoned, it was occupied by Americans in 1776. Some 1,700 British soldiers and their Indian allies advanced on the fort in 1777, but the garrison held out and set back their plans to seize the Hudson Valley.

Later that year, in two battles that changed the course of history, the British invasion of upstate New York was crushed on a battlefield within Saratoga National Historical Park. General John Burgoyne had advanced south along the Hudson River from Canada, relying on another British force to move north from New York City, but it never materialized. On Freeman Farm south of Saratoga (now Schuylerville), the British repelled the Americans on September 19. But in this war of attrition in a near-wilderness, the colonials, rallied by a still-loyal General Benedict Arnold, overpowered the British on October 7 on the same field of battle, and Burgoyne surrendered with 6,000 men on October 17. This demonstration of strength brought France into the war on the American side.

Further south, the Hudson flows past or near the homes of three presidents. Near Kinderhook, ex-President Martin Van Buren spent the last 21 years of his life at Lindenwald, a large two-story brick Georgian house. Its decorations featured 51 vividly colored wallpaper panels imported from France, and the property also included 220 acres of cropland, formal flower gardens, ornamental fish ponds, and wooded paths.

The birthplace and lifelong home of Franklin Delano Roosevelt overlooks the Hudson River near Hyde Park. To this rambling, often renovated house FDR brought his bride Eleanor in 1905 and here they raised their five children. The president called his office the Summer White House, and in that room in 1942 he and British Prime Minister Winston Churchill signed the agreement that resulted in the first atomic bomb. Franklin and Eleanor Roosevelt are buried nearby.

The Eleanor Roosevelt National Historic Site, on the grounds of the "big house," includes a cottage built in the 1920s for the use of Eleanor and two of her friends. She welcomed it as a place of retreat from her overbearing mother-in-law. After the president died and left their home to the American people, his widow continued to live at the cottage until her death in 1962.

Theodore Roosevelt was another president born not far from the Hudson River, on East 20th

The summer vacation home of Franklin Delano Roosevelt on Campobello Island, in Canada, adjacent to Maine. Misfortune struck the future president here in August 1921. After a vigorous day that included a swim in the icy waters of the Bay of Fundy, he became a victim of polio at the age of 39. This is now an international park.

The Saint-Gaudens National Historic Site in Cornish, New Hampshire, contains the home, studios, and gardens of Augustus Saint-Gaudens, America's foremost sculptor of the late 19th and early 20th centuries.

Saint-Gaudens' statues of military heroes and other figures projected an energetic, majestic appearance. An art colony formed in Cornish when friends and admirers of Saint-Gaudens came to New Hampshire to live and work near the sculptor.

Touro Synagogue, a national historic site in Newport, Rhode Island, is the oldest synagogue in the United States. One of the finest examples of colonial religious architecture, it is drawn from the models of classical antiquity.

Sephardic Jews from Spain and Portugal settled in Newport about 1658, and formed a congregation. Ground was broken for this synagogue in 1759. Congregation Yeshuat Israel—the Salvation of Israel— still worships in the synagogue.

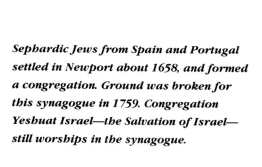

John Trumbull's painting of the surrender of General John Burgoyne at Saratoga commemorates a turning point in the Revolutionary War. The crushing defeat dealt to the British commander in upstate New York encouraged a hesitant France to intervene openly on the side of the Colonials.

The Schuyler House at Saratoga National Historical Park. General Philip Schuyler was commander of the American forces in the first of two critical battles fought against the British near Saratoga (now Schuylerville) in 1777. Fighting in a near-wilderness, Schuyler utilized a scorched earth policy against the invaders.

Street in Manhattan. Two other Park Service sites in the Empire State recall the life of "TR." The big Victorian structure of wood and brick called Sagamore Hill, in Oyster Bay on Long Island, was Roosevelt's home from the mid-1880s until his death in 1919. His second wife, Edith, died there in 1948. In Buffalo, at the Ansley Wilcox house, Vice President Roosevelt was sworn in as president on September 14, 1901, a few hours after President William McKinley died from an assassin's bullet.

The imposing statue of George Washington on the steps of Federal Hall in lower Manhattan marks the location of the inauguration of the first president in 1789. In northern Manhattan the magnificent tribute to President Ulysses S. Grant, the General Grant National Memorial, rises high above the Hudson River. Both he and his wife are buried in this immense shrine.

Elizabeth Cady Stanton (seated) initiated the women's rights movement in 1848 in Seneca Falls, New York. Stanton, who resented her husband's freedom while she was confined to caring for their children and managing their home, voiced her complaints to her friends. She and four other women called a convention to discuss women's rights. She is photographed here with Susan B. Anthony.

The Women's Hall of Fame in Seneca Falls, New York. The convention on women's rights in the town in 1848 adopted a list of grievances resembling those in the Declaration of Independence. The demand that women be given the right to vote was considered radical at the time.

Vanderbilt Mansion, now a historical site, was the home of members of one of America's wealthiest families. It is a representative example of the magnificent estates built along the Hudson River in upstate New York. The 54-room home, constructed of Indiana limestone, was completed in 1898.

The Louise Vanderbilt bedroom, the Vanderbilt Mansion. The Vanderbilts entertained lavishly in their home during the so-called Gilded Age. Their guests were neighbors of the same social class as well as nobility and leaders in business, politics, and the arts.

As governor of New York and then as president, Franklin Roosevelt sought out the tranquility of Hyde Park as often as possible as a respite from the turmoil of public life. Roosevelt, who died in 1945, gave the home to the American people.

Franklin Delano Roosevelt was born in this mansion at Hyde Park, New York, and he spent much of his life here. A child of wealth and privilege, Roosevelt nonetheless demonstrated, as few political leaders have, an appreciation for the problems of common people as well as a commitment to help by using the power of government.

Probably the most beloved of all of America's monuments is the Statue of Liberty in New York Harbor. Liberty Enlightening the World, the full name of this colossal sculpture, was a gift from France. It was conceived as a symbol of republicanism at a time when republican ideals were under attack in France. August Bartholdi, whose love of liberty was matched by his quest for grandeur in his art, had in mind such ancient statues as the Colossus of Rhodes. His unrivaled masterpiece, dedicated in 1886, stood rather well the test of time and the elements, but was refurbished before its centennial celebration in 1986.

At Edison National Historic Site in West Orange, New Jersey, one may see the laboratory and equipment used for 44 years by Thomas Alva Edison. Models of some of his inventions are on display. His 23-room house, Glenmont, contains original furnishings.

The wartime travails of the embattled young republic are recalled at Morristown National Historical Park in New Jersey. George Washington's Continental Army was encamped here for two winters, 1777 and 1779-80. The latter was especially severe, reportedly the worst winter of the century, in which the nearly starving and ill-clothed troops were assaulted by 28 blizzards. While the cold months were generally free of pitched battles, the colonists often skirmished with the British in the hope of capturing food. Smallpox claimed many lives, and desertions further thinned the ranks. Washington, demonstrating his brilliance as a leader, not only held his ragged forces together but prepared them for more battles to come.

This four-story brownstone on East 20th Street in Manhattan recreates the house where Theodore Roosevelt, the 26th president, was born in 1858. He spent his first 14 years here. His widow and sisters furnished the rooms to recall those years.

Sagamore Hill, on New York's Long Island, was built by Roosevelt in 1884 and 1885, and it was his permanent home for the rest of his life. Three of his children were born there. The president once wrote, "fond as I am of the White House... there isn't any place in the world like home."

Roosevelt was an energetic international hunter of big game, and a proud owner of many trophy heads and stuffed animals. But he was also the first president to work strongly in behalf of the protection of animal species in national wildlife refuges and parks.

Although his two terms as president were not considered a great success, Ulysses S. Grant, through his military skill, had preserved the Union, and this imposing tomb in New York City reflects the high esteem in which he was held.

LET
US HAVE
PEACE

The shot fired in Massachusetts and heard round the world resonated in Philadelphia, another hotbed of revolt and home of one of the dominant figures of the New World, Benjamin Franklin. A journalist, inventor, and urban planner, Franklin had helped make Philadelphia the most socially advanced city in the Colonies. Already nearly 70 when the First Continental Congress convened in Carpenters Hall in 1774, Franklin was also a leading advocate of independence and union among the Colonies.

The Congress addressed a declaration of rights and grievances to King George III. Up north, tensions turned to bloodshed in 1775, and in June 1776 a Virginia delegate to the Second Continental Congress, Richard Henry Lee, introduced a resolution declaring "That these United Colonies are, and of right ought to be, free and independent States." Congress passed the resolution and assigned a 33-year-old Virginian, Thomas Jefferson, to draft a Declaration of Independence.

Working alone, Jefferson composed perhaps the most eloquent proclamation ever written, in which he asserted that people everywhere have the right to be free and to be protected by a government chosen by the citizens of a nation. Congress, meeting in the State House (now Independence Hall), adopted the Declaration on July 4, 1776. Signing it, they dipped their quills in the silver inkstand still on display. The Declaration was read publicly for the first time in a park in front of the State House.

The U.S. Constitution was drafted in Independence Hall in 1787. Philadelphia was the seat of government of the new nation from 1790 to 1800, and the U.S. Supreme Court and the U.S. Congress met in buildings adjacent to Independence Hall. All of these shrines of liberty stand today, visited by millions, graceful in design to be sure, but above all symbolizing in their sturdy brick structure the strength of the institutions that were established here. A score of buildings and sites are part of Independence National Historical Park, one of the nation's most painstaking restorations and reconstructions. Blocks of dilapidated irrelevant buildings, more than 100 in all, were cleared from the immediate neighborhood to allow the edifices and the grassy and cobblestoned surfaces of 18th century Philadelphia to re-emerge.

Not to be overlooked is the Liberty Bell Pavilion, housing the bell that tolled the news of independence in 1776.

Almost lost in the artificial canyons of the Wall Street area of Lower Manhattan is Federal Hall, site of the original building where George Washington was sworn in as the first president. The first U.S. Capitol, birthplace of the Bill of Rights, was here.

Castle Clinton National Monument, a circular structure with an open-air center, has an unusually varied history. Originally a fort, it was built in 1811 to defend New York Harbor. It later served as a theater and an aquarium. The sculpture honors immigrants who entered the country through this building before Ellis Island was opened.

35

Facing the narrows of New York Harbor and the open sea beyond, the Statue of Liberty symbolizes to immigrants and other travelers the freedom and opportunity that they would find in the United States.

The feet of the Statue of Liberty before the immense figure (151 feet high, 225 tons) was assembled on an island in New York Harbor in 1886. The statue, a gift from France, has become a revered monument that, even in this era of nearby skyscrapers, dominates the harbor when seen from land, sea, or air.

"Tall ships" from many countries sailed into New York Harbor in 1986 to help salute the Statue of Liberty on the occasion of its 100th birthday. An extensive restoration of the statue had required several years of work.

Edison's bed at his West Orange laboratory. His library contained 10,000 volumes. His goal at West Orange was the "rapid and cheap development of inventions...useful things that every man, woman, and child wants...at a price they can afford to pay."

The Edison National Historic Site in West Orange, New Jersey preserves the laboratory and library of Thomas Alva Edison, one of America's most innovative geniuses. By the time he moved into West Orange from Menlo Park in 1887 at age 40 he had already invented the phonograph, the first practical incandescent lamp, and the distribution system to accompany it.

The Ford Mansion in Morristown, New Jersey was the headquarters for General George Washington during the winter of 1779-80. His army was encamped at nearby Jockey Hollow, where the soldiers suffered the ravages of disease, hunger, and an unusually cold winter.

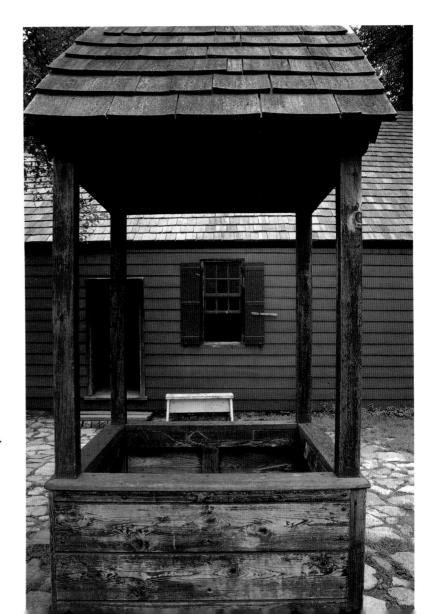

Edison's laboratory became a model for the modern private research and development lab in its success at linking business and technology. He once joked that he had on hand every conceivable substance his staff of 60 might need in their research, "from an elephant's hide to the eyeballs of a United States senator."

The well at the Wick House, Jockey Hollow. Some 1,000 simple huts were built nearby to house the 10,000 soldiers who trained and waited for warmer weather in which to resume the war.

Independence Hall, built in Philadelphia between 1732 and 1756, is the centerpiece of Independence National Historical Park. The graceful brick building was the Capitol of Pennsylvania. This complex of buildings served as the U.S. Capitol between 1790 and 1800, during most of George Washington's presidency.

Elfreth's Alley, with its quaint restored houses, is a step back in time to the 18th century, when Benjamin Franklin was the dominant figure in Philadelphia and the most famous man in the Colonies prior to the Revolution.

The clock tower at Independence Hall. The Second Continental Congress met here in 1775, after hostilities had broken out between Colonial soldiers and the British. Members of the Congress appointed George Washington as commander in chief of all Continental forces.

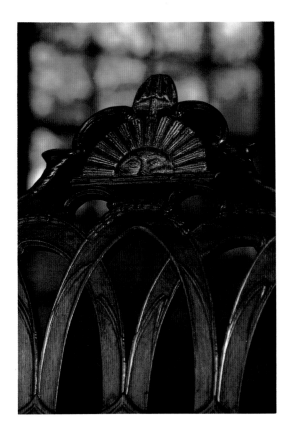

Valley Forge, 18 miles northwest of Philadelphia, was the site of the Continental Army's stressful but ultimately cathartic winter of 1777-78. Although no battle was fought here, the name Valley Forge has come to represent valor, suffering, and triumph over adversity. General George Washington chose the area, named after a forge along Valley Creek, where he could defend interior Pennsylvania from British raiding and foraging parties. Snow was on the ground when the army arrived on December 19, shoes already in tatters from long marches, and food soon became scarce. Often only firecake, a tasteless mixture of flour and water, provided nourishment. Pneumonia, typhoid, typhus, and dysentery claimed 2,000 lives.

The spirits and discipline of the soldiers were lifted after the arrival in February of Friedrich von Steuben, formerly of the elite General Staff of Frederick the Great of Prussia. His intensive daily drills whipped the army into fighting condition. Assembling on the Parade Ground on May 6, 1778, the army learned of the alliance with France. Emerging from the period of testing with new resolve and augmented with volunteers in the spring, the troops marched forth in June to contest the British on even terms.

Hopewell Furnace National Historic Site, a few miles northwest of Valley Forge, preserves the buildings and furnace of an iron-manufacturing enterprise that flourished from Revolutionary times until 1883. The social structure of this "iron plantation" of some 5,000 acres was somewhat similar to that of cotton plantations in the South. Presiding over all, usually from the "big house," was the owner of the furnace, though some owners employed an ironmaster. The latter controlled the lives of the villagers, while he and his family lived in the style of country squires. The furnace clerk supervised the company store and purchased materials for the industry. The "founder" operated the furnace. The vast majority of the villagers were workers and their families. Their lot was a dreary one, toiling 12 hours a day in the sweltering, grimy furnace.

This house in Philadelphia, the Thaddeus Kosciuszko National Memorial, is the smallest unit in the National Park System—0.02 acre. It honors a hero of the American Revolution who also devoted much of his life to the cause of freedom for his native Poland.

The Liberty Bell and a Park Service guide. Cast in 1752 in London, the iron bell weighs 2,080 pounds and has a circumference of 12 feet. From the State House (later Independence Hall) it rang out the news on July 8, 1776 that independence had been proclaimed. It eventually became damaged beyond repair.

Gettysburg, like Valley Forge, is a name filled with symbolism and meaning. The Civil War battle represented the high tide of the Confederacy, its farthest advance into the North. Military historians regard Gettysburg as the greatest battle fought on the American continent. The confrontation evolved from the determination of the Confederate commander, Robert E. Lee, that—after a string of victories in Virginia—it was time to carry the war to the North. A triumph there, with destruction of a large part of the Union army, could mean a loss of resolve that might bring a negotiated cessation of hostilities and independence for the Confederacy.

Lee was hampered when cavalry under J.E.B. Stuart rode far to the east and was lost to the Confederate assault. As with many battlefields, Gettysburg was a matter of coincidence—a place where chance skirmishing prompted more and more men under arms to converge on the scene. The opposing armies fought over ordinary places whose names acquired capital letters and became a part of the lore of the history of human combat. Over a three-day struggle, July 1, 2, and 3, 1863, involving various units of some 160,000 men on both sides, the Confederates won many fights—at the Wheat Field, the Peach Orchard, Devil's Den, Seminary Ridge—but lost the battle.

The climax came when Lee, realizing that supplies were short and he must withdraw or admit defeat, ordered a final charge against the Union line. The attack by 15,000 men across open terrain was a calamitous failure, and "Pickett's Charge" would thereafter be a synonym for courage and futility. Lee withdrew to the south the next day, his greatest opportunity behind him. Casualties on both sides totaled more than 43,000.

The author Edgar Allen Poe lived at this house in Philadelphia in 1843 and 1844. The sculpture recalls "The Raven," one of Poe's best known poems.

General Washington's headquarters at Valley Forge. The sacrifice by the soldiers was not in vain, for their presence west of Philadelphia kept the British bottled up in that city during the winter.

The Continental Army, encamped at Valley Forge during the winter of 1777-78, overcame hunger, disease, and bitterly cold weather, which claimed thousands of lives without a shot being fired. But the soldiers, rested and better trained, left their simple huts—these are reconstructions—in June 1778 to continue the fight for independence.

The Johnstown Flood, a tragedy of a far different kind that exacted a heavy toll of human life, occurred in Pennsylvania 26 years later. Fourteen miles upriver from Johnstown, a steel company town of 30,000, an earthen dam held back the waters of Lake Conemaugh, which was two miles in length. The South Fork Fishing and Hunting Club had repaired the 72-foot-tall dam carelessly and without the assistance of engineers.

Heavy rains on May 30 sent the level of the lake inching upward, and intensive but futile efforts were made to shore up the dam. At 3:10 p.m. on May 31 the dam broke. The flood of water and debris would not reach Johnstown for another 57 minutes, but power lines were knocked down and the populace received little warning—only a low rumble that built to a thunderous sound. Twenty million tons of water, 36 feet high and moving at a speed of 40 miles an hour, tore into the narrow valley in which the town stood. The water crushed whole blocks of buildings, and the debris and water then smashed additional structures with even more devastating force. The horror reached a climax at the old stone railroad bridge, where debris piled up along with 500 humans, many of whom were entangled in barbed wire from a destroyed wire plant. At that point the oily water caught fire, at a cost of another 80 lives.

The next morning, receding waters revealed a nearly leveled town and vast heaps of mud and

Craftsmen demonstrate the iron-making process at Hopewell Village for visitors. In this "company town," the owner of the furnace controlled the lives of the workers and their families.

47

The memory of those who have fought in the American Revolution and the Civil War is kept alive by 20th century citizens who re-create the battles that changed the course of history. These "Union soldiers" march at Gettysburg at the 125th anniversary re-enactment in July 1988.

The swirl and tumult of the Gettysburg Battlefield are captured in the Cyclorama created by Paul Phillippoteaux in 1884 and exhibited at the visitor center.

Other contemporary Americans assume the roles of Confederate soldiers at the re-enactment. The Southerners often needed clothing, and in fact it was a report that Gettysburg had a supply of shoes that sent rebel soldiers, many of whom were barefooted, toward the town of Gettysburg in the first place.

The firing of Union cannon during the re-enactment. This was the fire that responded to "Pickett's Charge" into the heart of the Union defensive line. A few Southerners reached the crest of Cemetery Ridge, only to be hurled back. Historian J.G. Randall wrote of the rebel attack, "As life poured out like water the flower of Southern manhood was sacrificed in a ghastly slaughter."

The Soldiers' monument at the Gettysburg National Cemetery stands near the spot where President Lincoln delivered his Gettysburg Address on November 19, 1863.

A view north from Little Round Top toward the central portion of the Gettysburg battlefield. Across these fields, on the afternoon of July 3, 1863, 15,000 men under General George Pickett marched into withering fire from Union defenders occupying the slightly higher ground of Cemetery Ridge.

Troops and citizens proceed toward the Gettysburg cemetery for the dedication ceremonies on November 19, 1863. In President Lincoln's address, a rhetorical masterpiece, he vowed "that these dead shall not have died in vain—that this nation, under God, shall have a new birth of freedom."

The Ridgely Mansion, Hampton National Historic Site, Towson, Maryland. Constructed in a wilderness between 1783 and 1790, this 33-room mansion is one of the most ornate Georgian houses in the United States. It was the centerpiece of a plantation worked by slaves until 1865.

Anticipating retirement, General and Mrs. Dwight Eisenhower purchased this farm on the edge of the Gettysburg battlefield in 1950. Their retirement plans were postponed for 10 years however, as "Ike" was to serve as NATO commander and later as president.

The dining room at the Eisenhower home. During Eisenhower's military career, he and Mamie had moved on average once a year, and this was their only permanent home.

A bygone era of travel is recalled at the Steamtown National Historic Site in Scranton, Pennsylvania. Steam locomotives, a roundhouse, and switchyards are among the exhibits.

The Ridgely family fortune, which made possible the Hampton Mansion, was based on iron and agriculture. Much of the ore, easily mined in the area, went into cannon and shot for the Continental army during the Revolution.

rubble. A total of 2,209 died, and 40 more fell victim to typhoid. The newly formed American Red Cross, led by Clara Barton, distinguished itself in the rescue effort. Today, tourists can visit a flood museum and see the abutments of the dam.

In Maryland, the British bombardment of Fort McHenry, in Baltimore Harbor, and its successful resistance would be remembered only as one of several American victories in the War of 1812, were it not for Francis Scott Key. The young lawyer had been detained by the British on a ship behind British lines in Baltimore Harbor on the night of September 13-14, 1814, because he had learned of plans for the attack on Baltimore. At dawn, Key saw the American flag still aloft over the fort, and later described his feeling: "Through the clouds of the war the stars of that banner still shone in my view, and I saw the discomfited host of its assailants driven back in ignominy to their ships."

Jotting down notes at once, Key composed a poem that was soon published and later set to music. The poem became the U.S. national anthem, "The Star Spangled Banner." The fort is now protected within Fort McHenry National Monument and Historic Shrine, and the flag that flew over the fort that night and caught Key's eye through the smoke of battle is preserved in the Smithsonian Institution in Washington, D.C.

Pleasant rolling green fields and low hills of central Maryland, just east of the Potomac River, were stained with the blood of 23,000 Americans on a September day in 1862. The battle of

The British fired some 1,500 to 1,800 rockets and shells at Fort McHenry in a 25-hour period ending shortly after dawn on September 14. The fort did not surrender, and the British threat to Baltimore was over.

Antietam (named for the creek that flows through the battlefield), or Sharpsburg (the South's name, for the town adjacent to the fighting), claimed a higher toll of casualties than any other one-day event in American history.

The battle itself was indecisive but its results were significant. The Confederate commander, General Robert E. Lee, in his first thrust toward the North, had marched into Maryland in search of badly needed men and supplies. His 41,000 men were confronted by 87,000 Union soldiers under General George McClellan, as the armies established lines on either side of the creek. The epic clash of arms began at dawn on September 17, but this was no finely orchestrated battle that went according to anyone's plan. Indeed, confusion reigned. For three hours soldiers fought back and forth across the Miller Cornfield, with the corn itself leveled as if by a knife, and, as Union General Joseph Hooker wrote, "the slain lay in rows precisely as they had stood in their ranks a few minutes before."

At midday, the action shifted southward, where McClellan's army attacked a half-mile stretch of the Sunken Road, thereafter known as The Bloody Lane. A survivor wrote that after the battle he could have walked on the road as far as he could see atop the bodies of the dead, without ever stepping on the ground.

The Chesapeake and Ohio Canal, built between 1828 and 1850, extends 184.5 miles along the Potomac River from Georgetown, in Washington, D.C. (shown here) to Cumberland, Maryland. The canal's 74 locks raise its waters from near sea level to an elevation of 605 feet.

The battle of Antietam, in Maryland, on September 17, 1862, was violent even by Civil War standards. The two armies suffered 23,000 casualties. For hours they fought along this sunken road, now known as The Bloody Lane. Bodies filled the roadbed.

Antietam National Cemetery, established in 1865, contains the graves of 4,776 Union soldiers.

Burnside Bridge, at Antietam, bears the name of General Ambrose Burnside, whose Union forces struggled for hours to cross the bridge against a fierce defense by Georgians holding heights to the right. Historians have noted that Burnside's soldiers could have waded across the creek.

Harpers Ferry, West Virginia, at the confluence of the Potomac and Shenandoah rivers, was an important stop on the way west before the Civil War. John Brown, a radical abolitionist who hoped to incite a slave rebellion, raided the town in 1859 and tried to seize weapons manufactured there. He and his followers were captured, and Brown was hanged.

Still further south, General Ambrose Burnside tried for hours to cross a bridge (now known as Burnside Bridge) over Antietam Creek, but Georgian defenders kept his men at bay. Burnside finally made it, only to be checked again, and Lee withdrew his army across the Potomac to safety. Lee's failure to win the battle caused Great Britain to delay recognizing the Confederacy, and President Abraham Lincoln took advantage of the ensuing lull in the fighting by issuing the Emancipation Proclamation, which declared free all slaves living in the Confederacy.

Harpers Ferry National Historical Park in West Virginia, Maryland, and Virginia embraces a town that has become a museum piece. A Federal arsenal was built at Harpers Ferry, West Virginia in 1796, and here many of the rifles and muskets used in the War of 1812 and the Civil War were manufactured. John Brown, a radical abolitionist, and his band of followers attacked the arsenal in 1859, intending to seize the weapons and give them to slaves who presumably would be prepared to fight for their freedom. But Brown was captured and hanged.

During the Civil War, Harpers Ferry, strategically situated at the confluence of the Shenandoah and Potomac rivers and nestled below the Blue Ridge, was fought over repeatedly by Union and Confederate forces. At one point the retreating Federals destroyed the arsenal. It was never rebuilt. The town, devastated by war, declined economically, but many of its historic buildings still stand, and it is being superbly restored for modern-day visitors.

Harpers Ferry's strategic location proved its undoing during the Civil War. The scene of many skirmishes througout the fighting, the town never was able to recover from the ravages of war and went into economic decline.

Today, Harpers Ferry remains frozen in time. Its permanent population is barely 400, but much of the old town still stands, and buildings are being restored. Nature trails, including the Appalachian Trail, lead to overlooks on the Blue Ridge.

WASHINGTON, D.C.

For two centuries the White House has served both as the official residence of the First Family and as the president's office. It has been the scene of many events of great importance to the United States and the world.

The Washington Monument, in its strength and simplicity, is a fitting tribute to George Washington. The 555-foot hollow marble obelisk weighs 90,000 tons. Its scale and form are based on obelisk designs from ancient Egypt.

The Jefferson Memorial was dedicated in 1943 on the 200th birthday of Thomas Jefferson, author of the Declaration of Independence and third president of the United States. The walls and dome are of white Vermont marble.

President Lincoln was seated in the flag-draped box at Ford's Theatre in Washington, D. C. on April 14, 1865, attending a performance of Our American Cousin. John Wilkes Booth, an actor and Southern sympathizer, entered the box from the rear unchallenged, and shot Lincoln fatally. As Booth leaped to the stage, he became entangled in the decorations for the presidential box and broke his leg. He then fled from the theatre.

I HAVE SWORN U

WE HOLD THESE TRUTHS TO BE SELF-EVIDENT; THAT ALL MEN ARE CREATED EQUAL, THAT THEY ARE ENDOWED BY THEIR CREATOR WITH CERTAIN INALIENABLE RIGHTS, AMONG THESE ARE LIFE, LIBERTY AND THE PURSUIT OF HAPPINESS, THAT TO SECURE THESE RIGHTS GOVERNMENTS ARE INSTITUTED AMONG MEN. WE··· SOLEMNLY PUBLISH AND DECLARE, THAT THESE COLONIES ARE AND OF RIGHT OUGHT TO BE FREE AND INDEPENDENT STATES···AND FOR THE SUPPORT OF THIS DECLARATION, WITH A FIRM RELIANCE ON THE PROTECTION OF DIVINE PROVIDENCE, WE MUTUALLY PLEDGE OUR LIVES, OUR FORTUNES AND OUR SACRED HONOUR.

Jefferson's statue within the memorial is 19 feet high. Four panels contain excerpts from his most eloquent writings. This quotation is from the Declaration of Independence.

The classical design of the Lincoln Memorial conveys the nobility and solemn dignity we associate with Abraham Lincoln. The colonnade of white Colorado marble is 189 feet long.

Lincoln is presented in a contemplative mood in this sculpture in Georgia marble. Flanking the statue are stone tablets containing the texts of his Gettysburg Address and his Second Inaugural Address.

Washington, D. C. is a nexus of living history. Events occur there daily that influence our lives. The city contains and displays to good advantage the nation's most outstanding assemblage of historic monuments.

The White House, by no means as imposing as the palaces of kings and queens, projects a quiet elegance befitting the world's oldest democracy. Its original design, dating from 1792, was never fully executed because of subsequent revisions and additions, but the Executive Mansion has aged gracefully and grown along with the breadth of responsibilities of its occupants. John Adams, the second president, and all of his successors have lived there, although James Madison was forced out after the British burned the White House in 1814, and Harry Truman vacated the building for four years while it was being restored. The East Room has seen many festive receptions and balls, but, as well, the bodies of seven presidents have lain in state there. The mansion's reputation as a repository for antiques and paintings dates from the redecoration undertaken by Mrs. John F. Kennedy.

Ford's Theatre National Historic Site commemorates the assassination of President Abraham Lincoln. John T. Ford, a theatrical entrepreneur, had opened the theatre in 1863. The performance of *Our American Cousin* on April 14, 1865, was an especially festive occasion because the Civil War had ended just five days earlier and because of the presence of President Lincoln and his wife. During the performance, the actor John Wilkes Booth, a Southern sympathizer, entered the presidential box, shot the president in the back of the head, and leaped to the stage. He then fled from the scene on horseback. Booth was pursued and killed in Virginia, and four of his fellow conspirators were hanged. Ford's Theatre has since been restored.

The home of Frederick Douglass, a leader of the emancipation movement, stands on heights overlooking the Anacostia section of Washington, D.C. Douglass purchased the large Victorian house, breaking a "whites only" covenant, and lived there for 18 years until his death in 1895. Douglass, who never went to school, fled slavery as a young man, educated himself, became an outspoken champion of freedom for blacks, and wrote the first volume of his autobiography while still the legal property of his master. Douglass was also an effective advocate of women's rights.

The Washington Monument, a 555-foot obelisk of Maryland marble, was 51 years in the making from concept to completion. In 1833 a society was organized by leading citizens of the Capital to plan a monument to honor George Washington. By 1848 enough money was in hand to begin construction. The cornerstone was laid, and the hollow, unadorned shaft raised to a height of about 150 feet in 1854. Then a political dispute, followed by the Civil War, stopped construction, which did not resume until 1880, this time with federal funds. The capstone was put in place in 1884. Because the marble used in the 1880s came from a different stratum, the monument displays two subtle but distinct colors.

The Jefferson Memorial is a fitting tribute to the many-sided genius who had special talent as an architect. The circular, colonnaded structure, which was dedicated in 1943, represents an adaptation of the Neoclassical style that Jefferson introduced in the United States and utilized in his designs for the Virginia State Capitol, the rotunda for the University of Virginia, and for his home,

Vietnam War veterans wanted a simple, strong, eloquent memorial for those who had died in the war. The winning design in a national competition was submitted by Maya Ying Lin, a 21-year-old student at Yale. She said, "The names would become the memorial," and the names of 58,000 who died are engraved in the black granite.

In 1984, two years after the Vietnam Veterans Memorial was dedicated, these figures were added. Frederick Hart said of his sculpture, "They wear the uniform and carry the equipment of war; they are young. The contrast between the innocence of their youth and the weapons of war underscores the poignancy of their sacrifice."

Monticello. The statue of Jefferson, 19 feet in height within the memorial, was sculptured by Rudulph Evans, winner of a nationwide competition. Some 650 cherry trees lining the Tidal Basin adjacent to the memorial were the gifts to the city of Washington from the city of Tokyo, Japan.

Within two years of the death of Abraham Lincoln, Congress approved the construction of a monument to the first martyred president. But the project languished until Congress approved the design by Henry Bacon in 1913, and work was begun a year later. Completed in 1922, this white marble building evokes the classical Greek ideals symbolized in the Parthenon, yet the architectural forms and styles have been adapted to memorialize an oustanding modern political leader. For example, the 36 columns honor the 36 states in the Union when Lincoln died. The colossal seated statue of the 16th president rises 19 feet. The design by Daniel Chester French required more than four years to execute.

Few, if any, tributes to those killed in battle have touched visitors more deeply than the Vietnam Veterans Memorial in Constitution Gardens near the Lincoln Memorial. Dedicated in 1982, the polished black granite walls bear the names of more than 58,000 American men and women who died in the war or who remain unaccounted for. By including no statement on the war itself, which was and remains controversial, the memorial focuses attention on the individual sacrifices of those who fought. Two years later, a life-size sculpture of three servicemen by Frederick Hart was installed. The $7 million cost of the memorial was raised through contributions.

THE SOUTHEAST

Jamestown, Virginia was the site of the first permanent English settlement in America. These are replicas of the ships that were tied to trees on a peninsula in the James River in 1607

The 105 settlers at Jamestown constructed a fort soon after they arrived. This is a reconstruction. The colonists struggled to survive in a seemingly limitless wilderness filled with wild animals and threatening Indians. Tobacco was the first product to provide real income.

Captain John Smith was the most effective leader of the Jamestown colony. After his capture by Indians, he earned their trust and was returned to the colony. Smith suffered a serious gunpowder burn in 1609 and returned to England. He never came back.

Pocahontas, daughter of the Algonkian chief Powhatan, participated in the ceremony in which her father made John Smith a subordinate chief. According to legend, she saved Smith from execution, but that may have been only a part of the ceremony. She later married another settler, John Rolfe, and converted to Christianity.

In a short distance of less than 20 miles, the Colonial Parkway in Colonial National Historical Park in Virginia links three landmark settlements of the colonial era—Jamestown, Williamsburg, and Yorktown.

In May 1607 three ships bearing 105 courageous settlers were tied to trees at the edge of a peninsula on a river that the settlers named the James. In this swampy, decidedly unhealthful location was established the first permanent English settlement in America. Their town, James Cittie, now called Jamestown, was also named after King James I of England. Shortages of food and water, Indian hostility, and frequent dissension among the settlers nearly ended the experiment more than once. In 1609-10, during the "starving time," 440 of Jamestown's 500 residents died. But the colony ultimately flourished, thanks in part to the marketing of tobacco, a product that James I deplored as "base and vile…dangerous to the lungs."

After serving as Virginia's seat of government for nearly a century, Jamestown gave way to Williamsburg, just five miles away. It was here that George Washington, Thomas Jefferson, Patrick Henry, and others rose to prominence. One of the great historical restorations of the nation, Williamsburg is privately owned and not a part of the National Park System.

And it was only eight miles east of Williamsburg, at Yorktown, that the last major battle of the American Revolution was fought. General Washington, concluding that he could not defeat the British in New York, moved his army in the fall of 1781 from the Hudson Valley to the Yorktown Peninsula, where the British under Lord Charles Cornwallis were firmly entrenched on strategic

The defeat of Lord Charles Cornwallis by George Washington at Yorktown in October 1781 ensured independence for the new nation. This cave was reportedly the last headquarters for Cornwallis under the intense bombardment by American and French batteries.

The Old Church Tower is the only standing 17th century ruin in Jamestown. Construction began in 1639, and it was used until 1750. After serving as the capital of Virginia for nearly a century, Jamestown yielded to Williamsburg and thereafter faded as a community.

heights overlooking the York River. The apparently strong British position became a trap after the
French fleet defeated the British in Chesapeake Bay and closed off an avenue of escape. A sudden
storm thwarted an attempt by Cornwallis to move his forces to the north bank of the York River
and to a route of retreat to the north. A fierce pounding by American and French cannons so
devastated the British defenses that Cornwallis surrendered with 7,000 men on October 19, essen-
tially ending the American Revolution.

Virginia, birthplace of so many Revolutionary leaders, saw more fighting during the Civil War
than any other state. The Federal capital, Washington, at Virginia's northern border, and the
Confederate capital, Richmond, at the heart of the state, are only 75 miles apart.

The war's first major encounter occurred just 20 miles west of Washington in July 1861. Union
General Irwin McDowell set his sights on the rail junction at Manassas, a link to Richmond. With
jaunty confidence, his army of 35,000 marched out of Washington, certain that one battle would
win the war. But these were raw recruits, who had signed up for just 90 days. Washington's elite
trailed the troops carrying picnic baskets, looking forward to watching the battle.

The reality of war, its noise, smoke, and screams of death, was another matter. The Confederate
army, led by Generals Beauregard and Johnston, checked the Union advance, and it was here that
Colonel Thomas Jackson earned his nickname "Stonewall" by rallying his troops to hold firm just
when it seemed that his line of soldiers would collapse. Some 900 men were killed at First Manassas (First Bull Run was the northern name for the battle), and as the defeated Federal troops

Washington's birthplace (1732) burned on Christmas Day in 1779, while he was leading the fight for independence. A reconstruction stands in George Washington Birthplace National Monument along the lower Potomac River.

Washington spent much of his youth at Mount Vernon, the home of his half brother. After the latter died, the future president acquired the plantation in 1754. Washington spent much time over the years enlarging the plantation and improving and expanding the mansion overlooking the Potomac. He died here in 1799.

The first major battle of the Civil War, Manassas, or Bull Run, occurred 20 miles west of Washington in July 1861. The Southern victory signaled that the Confederacy had far more resolve and military strength than the North had assumed. The Confederate General Thomas Jackson earned his nickname "Stonewall" when his firm stand helped turn the tide of battle.

Booker T. Washington, who was to become the nation's leading black educator, was born a slave southeast of Roanoke, Virginia in 1856. These buildings are reconstructions. After emancipation he took a job in a salt mine that began at 4 a.m. so that he could attend school later in the day. He worked his way through Hampton Institute and then founded Tuskegee Institute in Alabama.

Virginia bore the brunt of the Civil War, and many Confederate victories were won in the state. But in 1865, Union forces occupied Richmond, the Confederate capital, and General Lee surrendered to General Grant at Appomattox Court House in April. This is a reconstruction of the McLean House.

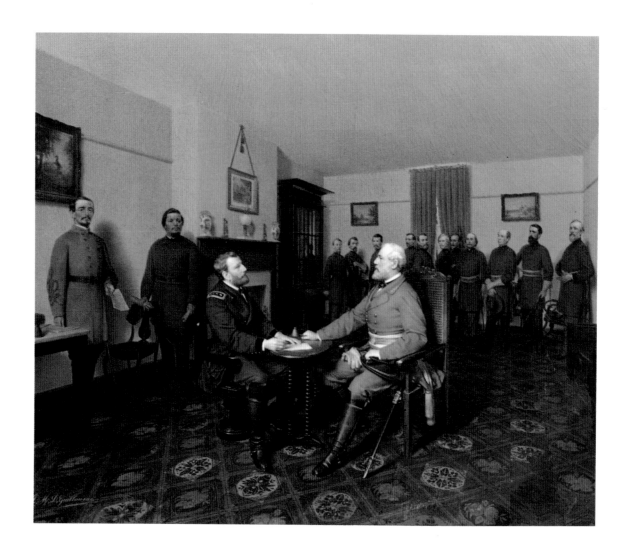

This painting depicts the surrender of Lee to Grant in the McLean House on April 9, 1865. The McLeans had moved from northern Virginia to get away from the war, only to have it end in their parlor.

streamed back into Washington, it was apparent that the war would not end soon. The opposing armies met again at Manassas in August 1862, and General Lee scored one of his greatest victories.

South of Manassas, battle-scarred landscapes abound. Fredericksburg/Spotsylvania National Military Park encompasses seven units. At Fredericksburg, in December 1862, repeated Union assaults on Lee's defenses atop heights above the Rappahannock River ended disastrously as Union soldiers were massacred by artillery and by infantry firing from behind a sunken road. Chancellorsville, another Southern victory in May 1863, ended in tragedy when Stonewall Jackson was shot in error by his own troops and mortally wounded. In the dense thickets and snarled undergrowth of the Wilderness, the armies fought in total confusion in May 1864 and set the woods ablaze with the fire from their weapons. A few days later, Spotsylvania saw the most intense hand-to-hand combat of the war.

At Petersburg, a desperate Confederate stand kept the Union forces at bay for ten months, but General Grant's army prevailed after the longest siege in American warfare, and Richmond was left virtually undefended. That city, which had withstood seven major offensives, was evacuated by Lee on April 2 1865. Grant found Richmond in flames, the Confederate government having authorized the burning of warehouses and supplies.

Two attempts in 1585 and 1587 to establish English colonies in America failed. The first settlers returned to England and the second contingent vanished and were never found. Both settlements were on Roanoke Island in North Carolina. The earthen fort built by the "Lost Colony" has been reconstructed.

Lee had reluctantly taken up arms against his country because he felt he owed primary allegiance to his home state of Virginia. His home of 30 years in Arlington, Virginia is being restored to its appearance when he and his wife, a great granddaughter of Martha Washington, lived there.

The United States Marine Corps War Memorial stands at the northern end of Arlington National Cemetery in Virginia. The bronze sculpture had its origins in the Pulitzer Prize-winning photograph by Joe Rosenthal of five Marines and a Navy hospital corpsman raising the American flag on Mount Suribachi on Iwo Jima during the fighting against the Japanese in February 1945.

WILBUR
WRIGHT
ORVILLE
WRIGHT

IN COMMEMORATION OF THE CONQUEST OF THE AIR

Lee, retreating westward, was soon overtaken by Grant at Appomattox Court House and, although several Confederate armies remained in the field, the Civil War effectively ended on April 9, 1865 with his surrender there. Under Grant's generous terms, soldiers who had worn the Gray had only to pledge not to take up arms against the United States again. Any Confederate soldier who owned a horse was allowed to take it home. Lee's Army of Northern Virginia, still 28,231 in number after the long and agonizing conflict, formally surrendered April 12. With many original structures still standing, the village of Appomattox has been restored to its appearance in 1865.

Twenty-two years before the landing at Jamestown, the English attempted to establish a settlement in present-day North Carolina, but it ultimately vanished, and the tragedy has remained a mystery. An expedition dispatched by Sir Walter Raleigh, a close friend of Queen Elizabeth I, in 1584 had reported finding a "most pleasant and fertile ground," and in 1585, with the Queen's and Raleigh's support, 108 colonists were transported to Roanoke Island, a serene place sheltered from the ocean by the Outer Banks. After managing to antagonize the Indians, the colonists elected to return to England.

The colony was reestablished in 1587, and the birth of Virginia Dare, the first English child born in America, seemed propitious. But when Governor John White returned from a trip to England in 1591, the 116 settlers had vanished from the face of the earth, leaving only the notation "Croatoan," the name of another island, carved on a post. No trace of the inhabitants was ever found there—or anywhere else.

Just five miles northeast of Fort Raleigh, on sand dunes at Kill Devil Hills, a far more successful experiment occurred in December 1903—the first gasoline-powered flight by a heavier-than-air craft. A gray granite shaft honors Orville and Wilbur Wright, inventors of the airplane.

Four units of the Park System in South Carolina commemorate battles at Fort Moultrie, Kings Mountain, the Village of Ninety-Six, and Cowpens that were critical to the outcome of the Revolutionary War. Cowpens, in particular, was a decisive victory for the Colonials.

The first shots of the Civil War were fired at these Federal fortifications at Fort Sumter, South Carolina, on April 12, 1861. For 34 hours the Confederate batteries pounded the masonry fort with shot and shell, after which the Federals agreed to evacuate. The South held this strategic position, guarding Charleston Harbor, for the next four years.

Ocmulgee National Monument in Georgia contains a site occupied by humans for 10,000 years. The earliest people were Ice Age hunters. From A.D. 900 to 1100 farmers lived here, raising corn, beans, squash, pumpkins, and tobacco in the bottomlands.

Fort Sumter National Monument (which includes Fort Moultrie), contains the shoal in Charleston Harbor where the first shots of the Civil War were fired on April 12, 1861. Confederate batteries ringing the harbor opened fire, with guns and mortars, on the Federal-controlled fort. The Federal commander agreed to evacuate on April 14. On April 15 President Lincoln called out 75,000 militia and the war was on in earnest.

Civil War sites in Georgia include Fort Pulaski, at the mouth of the Savannah River. With its heavy masonry walls, Fort Pulaski seemed impregnable, and its Confederate occupants were lulled into a false sense of security. From nearby Tybee Island, Federal troops under U.S. Captain Quincy Gillmore, an engineer, opened fire on the fortress, using a new weapon of war, rifled cannon, whose projectiles tore through Pulaski's walls with devastating effect. Pulaski's defenders surrendered the next day, and the North occupied the fort for the rest of the war. The successful siege signaled the end of old-style masonry fortifications.

Chickamauga and Chattanooga National Military Park in Georgia and Tennessee preserves sites of battles critical to the outcome of the Civil War. In August 1863 Union forces under General William Rosecrans closed in on the strategic rail center of Chattanooga, Tennessee. The Confederate commander, General Braxton Bragg, withdrew from the city in good order and crossed into Georgia. Rosecrans, believing this to be a demoralized retreat, pursued too carelessly, and a reinforced Confederate army repelled him in unusually bloody fighting in dense woods near West Chickamauga Creek that claimed 34,000 casualties in two days. Coming after defeats elsewhere, Chickamauga lifted Confederate spirits.

Rosecrans then withdrew to Chattanooga and Bragg followed and laid siege. He held high ground above the city on Missionary Ridge and Lookout Mountain. Union food and supplies ran short, but General Grant arrived and opened a supply route. In late November his forces attacked and captured Lookout Mountain in the so-called Battle Above the Clouds. General George Thomas successfully attacked Confederate rifle pits at the base of Missionary Ridge. And then, without orders from Grant or Thomas, the soldiers assaulted the ridge itself. In one of the great infantry charges of the war, Thomas' men wrested control of the ridge from Confederate troops, thereby

Barracks at Fort Pulaski, a Confederate stronghold at the onset of the Civil War. The fort stood at the mouth of the Savannah River, in Georgia, and it was not thought that a Union assault could breach its thick masonry walls.

The people who lived at Ocmulgee a thousand years ago constructed a series of earth mounds. The interior of their earthlodge looked something like this.

Some of the destruction at Fort Pulaski in April 1862. Union forces on nearby Tybee Island were commanded by an engineer, Captain Quincy Gillmore, whose arsenal included ten new experimental rifled cannon. Their projectiles tore through Pulaski's walls, forcing the fort's surrender, and ended the era of stone and brick fortifications.

Brotherton Cabin, as it was in 1863, during the battle of Chickamauga south of Chattanooga, Tennessee. When a Union division withdrew from the battle line by mistake, Southerners pushed through at this spot and won the battle.

After their victory at Chickamauga, Confederates were confident they could recapture Chattanooga, a key rail center. They held these heights above the city and imposed a siege. But General Ulysses S. Grant opened a supply route from the north, and Union soldiers, utilizing a heavy fog as cover, successfully assaulted the mountain.

Gate at Point Park, Lookout Mountain. After the mountain fell to the North, Union forces charged up nearby Missionary Ridge without waiting for orders, captured those heights, and ended the siege of Chattanooga. This victory opened the way for the advance on Atlanta.

securing eastern Tennessee for the Union and opening the heartland of the South to further attack. It was from Chattanooga that General William Sherman began his advance on Atlanta in 1864.

Andersonville National Historic Site in southern Georgia is a memorial to all Americans ever held as prisoners of war in any war. Some 45,000 Union prisoners were held at Andersonville during the Civil War. The Confederate government was unable to provide adequate food, clothing, and medical care, and as a result 12,912 men died while interned. The Andersonville National Cemetery contains more than 16,000 graves.

In Atlanta, the Martin Luther King, Jr., National Historic Site includes the birthplace, church, and grave of Dr. King. The civil rights leader gained much of his fame from the inspiring sermons he delivered at the Ebenezer Baptist Church. The gravesite of the martyred black advocate of nonviolence is next to the church.

Some of the nation's earliest recorded history is recalled at historic sites in Florida. The De Soto National Memorial, in Bradenton, commemorates the four-year (1539-1543) exploration of the Southeast by Hernando de Soto of Spain. He discovered the Mississippi River, but not the gold he wanted so badly, and died in the process.

Fort Caroline, in Jacksonville, has been reconstructed on the basis of a 16th century sketch. Here, French Huguenot (Protestant) colonists, fleeing brutal religious persecution, settled in 1564, but the fort was captured by Spaniards in the following year. Thirty-five miles to the south, the Spaniards founded St. Augustine, the oldest city in the United States, in 1565. After the first nine forts they built there, all wooden, succumbed to fire, humidity, and shoddy construction, they began construction in 1672 of Castillo de San Marcos, a massive stone fort.

The equestrian figures of three Confederate leaders have been carved on the sheer granite face of Stone Mountain, outside Atlanta, Georgia. The subjects are President Jefferson Davis, General Robert E. Lee, and General Thomas (Stonewall) Jackson. Work on the sculpture began in 1923 and, after a long interruption, it was completed in 1970.

Martin Luther King, Jr., a Baptist preacher who adopted the precepts of nonviolence practiced by Mahatma Gandhi, emerged in the 1950s as the leader of the black civil rights movement in the United States.

King's achievements are memorialized in a national historic site in Atlanta that includes his birthplace and the Ebenezer Baptist Church where he was co-pastor with his father. King, who won the Nobel Peace Prize, was assassinated in 1968. His tomb is near the church.

Another impressive fortification, Fort Jefferson, occupies one of the Dry Tortugas, an island chain almost 70 miles west of Key West in the Gulf of Mexico. Fort Jefferson National Monument encompasses the seven islands of the Dry Tortugas. The fort was built by the U.S. government in 1846, but was never tested in battle because the development of rifled cannon had rendered brick and masonry forts obsolete. Instead, it became a prison for army deserters. Dr. Samuel Mudd, linked to the plot to kill Abraham Lincoln because he gave medical aid to John Wilkes Booth, the president's assassin, was imprisoned here. He was pardoned in 1869 after rendering assistance during a yellow fever epidemic.

Few places in the world were occupied by humans for a greater length of time than Russell Cave. From 7000 B.C. until A.D. 1000 Native Americans lived in the cave near Bridgeport, Alabama. In bands of 15 or so they sought warmth, shelter, and water in this cavern 4,000 years before the Egyptians built the Great Pyramids. The earlier visitors hunted wild game and collected edible plants, and later on their descendants may have practiced agriculture. Bone tools, pottery, graves, and other artifacts examined by archaeologists at Russell Cave National Monument tell an incredible story of human survival.

A rarity in the National Park System, an institution of higher education, has been made a national historic site. Tuskegee Institute in Alabama was founded by Booker T. Washington in 1881 at a time of declining fortunes for black Americans. With segregation on the rise and opportunities for advancement few and far between, Washington sought to train teachers who in turn would fan out across the South and educate other blacks. Students at Tuskegee also acquired skills needed to earn a living in the trades and in agriculture. Washington's exemplary moral leadership and his skill

The Castillo de San Marcos in Florida, constructed from 1672 to 1695, is the oldest stone fortress in the nation. It was built by the Spanish to protect St. Augustine, the oldest city (founded 1565) in the United States.

The reconstructed fortifications of Fort Caroline, overlooking the St. Johns River in present-day Jacksonville, Florida, represent a short-lived attempt by French Huguenots to establish a settlement in 1564, 43 years before the first permanent English settlement in the future United States. Spaniards destroyed the colony in 1565.

The Spanish constructed this watchtower, now designated Fort Matanzas National Monument, at the mouth of the Matanzas River in 1742 to protect the southern approach to Saint Augustine. Matanzas is Spanish for "slaughters." More than 200 French Huguenot prisoners were killed at the site by the Spanish in 1565.

Fort Jefferson is in the national monument by the same name, one of the most isolated park units in the "lower 48" states. Accessible by seaplane, the fort stands in the midst of the Gulf of Mexico. The seven islands of the Dry Tortugas are in the monument. "Tortuga" is Spanish for turtle, which the Spanish found in plentiful supply. These dry islands have no fresh water.

Fort Jefferson was built to protect American shipping in the Gulf of Mexico. Designed to accommodate 450 guns, the fort was never finished. Black slaves and then, during the Civil War, Union deserters, were put to work on its construction.

Small bands of Native Americans first ventured into this cavern in Alabama nine millennia ago. Now protected within Russell Cave National Monument, the cavern provided warmth and water to humans for 8,000 years, until A.D. 1000. Few places in the world have such a long history of cultural evolution; early occupants were nomadic hunters and gatherers, but the more recent ones lived in nearby villages where they grew corn and other crops.

Tuskegee Institute, in Tuskegee, Alabama, a milestone in black education, was founded by Booker T. Washington. Classes began in a dilapidated church and shanty in 1881, but the school went on to gain international recognition.

Students attend a writing class in Tuskegee Institute in 1902. The school, now a national historic site, brought hope through education to the children of slaves in the decades after the Civil War.

at winning financial support from prominent citizens made the school a spectacular success.

The George Washington Carver Museum at the Institute honors the former head of the agriculture department who, through research, developed more than 300 products from peanuts and sweet potatoes, including plastics, dyes, medicines, and fertilizers.

Tennessee, though a member of the Confederacy, was in fact sharply divided in its loyalties during the Civil War. Three battles in the state figured prominently in the eventual Union victory. The first major victory for the North occurred in February 1862 with the capture of Fort Donelson on the Cumberland River. This was the first major test for Ulysses S. Grant, who would emerge as the overall Union commander after several other generals chosen by President Lincoln failed to meet the tests of leadership.

Fought in April 1862, the Battle of Shiloh, the fiercest in the United States up to that time, was another victory for Grant. Grant's triumph secured western Tennessee for the Union, and opened the way for the assault on Vicksburg, which would result in a geographical division of the Confederacy. Stones River, site of a midwinter battle from December 31, 1862 to January 2, 1863, was indecisive but signaled the onset of a Federal move to split the Confederacy yet again, this time in the Southeast.

Vicksburg National Military Park, in Mississippi, embraces the site of a major Union victory. The fall of this Confederate bastion, after a 47-day siege, gave Union forces control of the Mississippi River, and cut the Confederacy in two. Previous Union efforts to take the city had failed, but the strategy devised by General Grant succeeded. The surrender of the city, on July 4, 1863, one day after the Union victory at Gettysburg, was the turning point in the war and foreshadowed ultimate Confederate defeat.

Shiloh, the scene of a Union victory in southwestern Tennessee in April 1862, was a chaotic clash of young recruits. Most had never heard a shot fired in anger and had received little or no training. One soldier, explaining how to load and fire, told his comrades, "It's just like shooting squirrels, only these squirrels have guns, that's all."

Union dead are buried at the National Cemetery at Shiloh. The Confederate dead lie in five marked trenches. Killed in the spring of their lives, the soldiers fell on an April battlefield where bullets clipped peach trees and showered the ground with pink blossoms.

The Confederates made a strong stand on the bluffs above Vicksburg, but General Grant, in a bold stroke, crossed the river from the west, circled the city from the south, cut off rail connections, and forced the city to surrender after a 47-day siege. Some 1,400 monuments, memorials, and tablets tell the story of the conflict at Vicksburg National Military Park.

William T. Sherman, the Union general, called the Mississippi River "the spinal column of America." A major Union objective during the Civil War was to sever that column and split the Confederacy by capturing Vicksburg, Mississippi. This view is from Confederate positions at Vicksburg.

Two other battlefield sites in Mississippi, Brices Cross Roads and Tupelo, recall the brilliance of the Confederate General Nathan Bedford Forrest, the war's ablest cavalry commander, who made Union forces advancing in the South in 1864 pay dearly.

The Jean Lafitte National Historical Park and Preserve in Louisiana is one of the most diverse units in the Park System. The Chalmette unit, seven miles east of New Orleans, embraces the site of the Battle of New Orleans, the climactic clash of the War of 1812, and the last time that Americans fought Englishmen. Advancing from the East, the British sought to capture New Orleans and hence gain control of the mouth of the Mississippi River, which would have threatened the economy of the entire Mississippi Valley and slowed U.S. westward expansion. But on January 8, 1815, an attack on defenses put up by General Andrew Jackson proved to be a disaster. In a battle lasting less than 30 minutes, the British were thrown back with 2,000 casualties, against an American loss of 13. The military triumph ultimately propelled Andrew Jackson into the White House.

Judge Isaac Parker served this court for 21 years. The gallows at Fort Smith National Historic Site recall his nickname, "the hanging judge." He dealt sternly with frontier lawlessness, which was especially rampant in the Indian Territory west of Fort Smith. He handled 13,500 cases, and sentenced 79 felons to death by hanging.

Fort Smith, an army post in Arkansas from 1817, was abandoned by the War Department in 1871. The settlement then served as U.S. District Court for western Arkansas and the Indian Territory. The barracks was converted into a courtroom.

Centuries ago, Native Americans bathed in the hot springs in Arkansas. The springs were neutral territory, where warring opponents relaxed in peace. The 47 springs are now within a national park, and water from all but two of them is channeled to bathhouses where visitors can luxuriate and hope for possible medical benefits. This grand bathhouse was built in the heyday of the springs' popularity.

The French Quarter is renowned for its food, music, and night life, often a bit on the wild side. Mardi Gras, which takes place in late winter of each year, is perhaps the gaudiest and least inhibited public celebration in the United States.

The oldest part of New Orleans is the French Quarter, or Vieux Carré, but its cultural heritage is Spanish as well as French. Many structures built by the French were leveled by fires in the 18th century. Houses have balconies of wrought iron, finely and superbly designed.

The historical park also encompasses one of the nation's great urban treasures, the French Quarter of New Orleans, the original part of the city. By no means an anachronism, the French Quarter is the heart of modern New Orleans, where thousands of people from all walks of life reside amid iron-decorated architectural museum pieces. Another unit of the park, south of the city, highlights the ecology of the Mississippi Delta and features bayous, freshwater swamps, and marshes.

Pea Ridge National Military Park in northwest Arkansas preserves one of the westernmost of the important Civil War battles. The Union victory here in March 1862 ensured that Missouri, a border state, would stay in the Union. The Confederate attack included two regiments of Cherokee Indians. The South withstood a Union counterattack until ammunition ran low and forced their withdrawal.

THE MIDWEST

The Gateway Arch, designed by Eero Saarinen, is the centerpiece of the Jefferson National Expansion Memorial in St. Louis. Rising 630 feet, the stainless steel arch was constructed between 1963 and 1965. The memorial park, situated alongside the Mississippi River, honors the 19th century pioneers, many of whom passed through St. Louis on their way west.

The Mount Rushmore faces are one of the world's largest sculptures. Gutzon Borglum achieved remarkable likenesses of the presidents. George Washington represents the founding of the nation, Thomas Jefferson the idea of representative government, Theodore Roosevelt the conservation of natural resources and the rise of America in world affairs, and Abraham Lincoln the preservation of the Union and equality for all.

THE CONQUEST OF THE WEST ★ GEORGE RO

The George Rogers Clark Memorial in Vincennes, Indiana. From their fort in Detroit, the British controlled the Old Northwest (Ohio, Indiana, Illinois, Michigan, and Wisconsin) at the outset of the American Revolution. Clark, a young Virginian, changed that and opened the Midwest to the new nation.

Mounds built by ancient Indians for religious and burial purposes have long fascinated archaeologists in the Midwest and South. This is the Mound City Group National Monument in Ohio.

America's first great naval victory occurred in Lake Erie during the War of 1812, when Admiral Oliver Hazard Perry defeated the British fleet and took six ships captive, an astonishing coup against the world's premier seapower. Perry then sent his famous message, "We have met the enemy and they are ours." A 352-foot granite shaft on South Bass Island (a part of Ohio) commemorates Perry's victory.

Ohio was also the home of six presidents, and two of them, James A. Garfield and William Howard Taft, are remembered in Park Service units.

Abraham Lincoln was a man of America's heartland, and memorials in the states of Kentucky (where he was born), Indiana (where he grew up), and Illinois (where he lived as an adult) commemorate the life of the Great Emancipator.

The heaviest casualty toll—some 2,500 soldiers—of any Civil War battle fought west of the Mississippi River occurred at Wilson's Creek, now a national battlefield, in southwestern Missouri in August 1861. The Confederates won the battle but were unable to pursue the Union force, and hence were unable to bring Missouri into the Confederacy.

That same summer, 45 miles to the west, George Washington Carver was born. While an infant, he and his mother and brother were seized by Confederate bushwackers. His mother disappeared, and his father's identity remains unknown, but the boys were purchased and raised by the Carvers. In frail health, and unable to do hard work, George turned his interest to plants and that led to a career as a botanist and agronomist. His birthplace site is now a national monument.

Thirty miles north of Carver's birthplace, and 23 years later, Harry Truman was born in Lamar, Missouri. Also rising from humble beginnings, Truman became the 33rd president of the United States. His home in Independence is a national historic site.

The Gateway Arch in St. Louis salutes the westward-bound pioneers of the 19th century. In Iowa, also along the western bank of the Mississippi River, are traces of a far earlier culture. Mounds, some shaped like animals and birds, extend for six miles atop bluffs above the river. The Effigy Mounds National Monument preserves these remains of a society that flourished between 500 and 2,500 years ago.

Pipestone National Monument, in Minnesota, contains the quarries from which Native Americans obtained materials for making ceremonial pipes. Pipestone is also known as Catlinite, for George Catlin, the artist, who visited the quarries in 1836 and wrote about them.

Two historic forts in Kansas recall the adventure of the frontier. Established in 1842, Fort Scott was manned by Dragoons, the elite troops of the frontier army, trained to fight either on foot or horseback. The colorfully dressed Dragoons, sporting sabers, fought valiantly in the Mexican War. Fort Larned was established in 1859 to protect mail and travelers heading west on the Sante Fe Trail.

Abraham Lincoln was born near Hodgenville, Kentucky, in 1809. This cabin, now within a massive marble and granite memorial, is believed to be his birth cabin. The future president was named for his grandfather, who had been slain by Indians. Abraham's father, Thomas, was a carpenter and farmer.

The Lincoln Boyhood National Memorial in southern Indiana contains a reconstructed homestead on the farm where the Lincolns lived from 1816 to 1830, when Abraham was 7 to 21 years old. Lincoln's father hacked out a road to the land he had claimed. Abraham helped clear the land and raise crops.

The granite peaks of the Black Hills in South Dakota were thrust up 60 million years ago, and since then wind and water have eroded and shaped the mountains. But a new kind of sculpturing occurred on Mount Rushmore between 1927 and 1941, when four gigantic heads of American presidents were blasted and carved out of the rock. The work, mostly covered by appropriations from the U.S. government, was done under the supervision of Gutzon Borglum and then his son Lincoln Borglum. Each face is 60 feet high. The heads are on an outcropping of rock 400 feet above the visitor center.

Fort Union Trading Post National Historic Site in North Dakota recalls a brief era in relations between Native tribes and white entrepreneurs. Established in 1829 by John Jacob Astor's American Fur Company, Fort Union was one of a number of posts along the upper Missouri River where the Blackfeet, Crow, and Assiniboins could trade beaver furs and buffalo hides. Contrary to some accounts, the Natives were hard bargainers, and competition was keen among the posts. The arrival of white men spelled misery for the Natives. Liquor devastated the tribes, and smallpox epidemics—the Natives possessed no natural immunity—killed thousands.

Four panels at the visitor center at the Boyhood Home depict Lincoln's life. Abraham's mother, who died when he was nine, is buried nearby. In Indiana Lincoln acquired a love for reading and a desire for education and knowledge.

Drawn by reports of rich black soil, the Lincolns moved to Illinois in 1830. Abraham soon struck out on his own, studied law, and was elected to the state legislature. He married Mary Todd in 1842. In 1844 they purchased this home in Springfield, the state capital, the only house they ever owned.

Lincoln's desk in his Springfield home. Because of his reputation for integrity, intelligence, and hard work, Lincoln gained respect from others, and in the 1840s he served a term in the U.S. House of Representatives.

The Lincolns had four sons, though only one would survive to maturity. In 1856 the home was expanded. When nominated for president in 1860, Lincoln campaigned from the front door of his home, greeting delegations of dignitaries and citizens.

After Lincoln was assassinated, his body was brought back to Springfield, and he was buried in Oak Ridge Cemetery. This monument also contains the crypts of Mrs. Lincoln and three of their sons.

Harry Truman lived in this Victorian house in Independence, Missouri, from his marriage to Bess Wallace in 1919 until his death in 1972. While he was president it was called the Summer White House.

The Herbert Hoover National Historic Site in West Branch, Iowa includes the cottage where the president was born in 1874. A blacksmith shop similar to his father's is here, as are the Friends meetinghouse where the Hoovers worshipped, a presidential library, and the graves of Hoover and his wife.

The boyhood home of Dwight Eisenhower in Abilene, Kansas. The future general and president was one of seven sons. Their hard-working parents were devout, conservative Christians. The Eisenhower Presidential Library is also in Abilene.

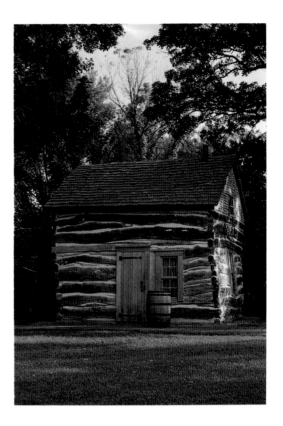

Rising 800 feet over the valley floor, Scotts Bluff in western Nebraska is both a natural and historical monument. Containing volcanic ash, sandstone, and siltstone, Scotts Bluff records 60 million years of earth history. It was a landmark on the Oregon Trail, traversed by some 350,000 pioneers between 1841 and 1869.

In Homestead National Monument, in southeastern Nebraska, an early cabin built under provisions of the Homestead Act of 1862. The law said anyone could get free land from the public domain by paying a small filing fee, building a house, and cultivating the land for five years. The appeal of free land sent Americans swarming westward.

Theodore Roosevelt, a New Yorker, established a cattle ranch in North Dakota, and the Maltese Cross Cabin was his home in 1884 and 1885. His years in the West infused the future president with a concern for protecting wildlife and wild lands. His ranch is now included in Theodore Roosevelt National Park.

THE WEST

"The Alamo," more accurately San Antonio de Valero, a Spanish mission founded along the San Antonio River in 1718. After its abandonment a century later, it entered Texas folklore when Texas declared its independence from Mexico in 1836. One hundred eighty three defenders of this mission-fortress volunteered to fight to the death—and they did—when the Mexicans attacked.

White House Ruin, one of the most photographed ruins in the country, in its awesome setting near the base of a striped cliff in Canyon de Chelly, Arizona. The canyon is a museum of ancient history. The White House section of the ruin is a façade covered with white plaster.

106

Mission San José is one of the four Spanish frontier missions preserved within the Park System in San Antonio. Here, as at other missions, Native Americans were introduced to the Roman Catholic Church.

Mission Concepción in San Antonio Missions National Historical Park. Now serene islands in a bustling city, these missions once stood in isolated splendor on the vast, dry plains of Texas.

The LBJ ranch in the hill country of central Texas represents the culmination of a frontier success story. Lyndon B. Johnson was born poor, but by combining entrepreneurial and political skills he achieved such success that he died a wealthy man, with a big spread across his ancestral homeland. Johnson was president from 1963 to 1969.

One of the loveliest groupings of historic buildings within the National Park System is found in San Antonio Missions National Historical Park. The missions have their foundations in the clash of empires in the 17th century. With Spain, England, and France eyeing the riches of the new world, Spain proved to be the most effective in using religion as an implement for advancing its national goals. The Spanish established Roman Catholic missions throughout the Southwest and California. Here, Native Americans were instructed on techniques of agriculture and in the teachings of Christ, and their loyalty to the Spanish crown was secured—at least that was the plan. These outposts shaped the Spanish culture that enriches the American Southwest today. Four missions in San Antonio are included in the historical park.

Fort Davis, in a lonely expanse of West Texas, guarded emigrants and stagecoaches along the San Antonio-El Paso Road between 1854 and 1891. Indian attacks were a serious problem. When the fort was abandoned, some 50 adobe and stone buildings remained standing, and the fort is regarded as the best preserved of its kind in the Southwest.

Westward from central Texas the climate becomes drier and the land gradually changes character. Areas of higher elevation, to the extent that they punctuate the horizon at all, are now angular rather than rounded, more often bare rather than wooded or grassed.

Man-made monuments from the distant past come from the land itself, and their survival reflects the strength of stone and mortar and the care of the craftsmen—and, of course, the arid climate.

In the Southwest prehistoric construction attained its highest expression in large apartment

Pueblo Bonito at Chaco Culture National Historical Park in New Mexico. The Anasazi flourished here a thousand years ago, and Pueblo Bonito, once four stories high, was the largest apartment complex in the United States until the late 19th century. This dwelling had 600 rooms and 40 kivas, or ceremonial structures.

An interior passageway at Pueblo Bonito. The craft of masonry was refined over the centuries as the pueblo buildings grew larger and higher. Some walls had inner cores of rubble faced with veneers of stone. Others consisted primarily of sandstone blocks chinked with stones.

houses lining Chaco Wash, a shallow, intermittent, yet life-giving stream that meanders across northwestern New Mexico. This area was occupied by the Anasazi, or "ancient ones," whose culture at Chaco reached its zenith around A.D. 1100. Thereafter they declined and disappeared from this vicinity altogether around 1200.

The Anasazi, who were farmers, occupied some 75 villages, and more than 400 miles of connecting roads have been identified. The most impressive ruins are preserved within Chaco Culture National Historical Park.

Aztec Ruins National Monument lies 65 miles north of the major pueblos at Chaco Canyon. The name is a misnomer, because the Aztecs of Mexico never circulated this far north.

The pueblos at Chaco and Aztec were built on broad open terrain, but those who settled above the Rio Grande, further east, chose steeper but greener country. In Frijoles Canyon in Bandelier National Monument the ancients grew corn, beans, and squash. The lava and consolidated volcanic ash are soft rocks that have been easily eroded and provide a dramatic scenic setting.

Two other national monuments in New Mexico, Pecos and Salinas, contain ruins of both ancient cultures and more recent Spanish missions. Nomadic Indians may have entered the Salinas Valley as long as 20,000 years ago. Successive cultures appeared in the area, but by A.D. 1300, Anasazi influence was dominant, and the large stone complexes found elsewhere were also built here. In this park are four of the six remaining Franciscan mission churches dating from the 17th century.

Arizona also contains a rich archaeological record of long-departed though not necessarily failed civilizations. Indeed people who abandoned the many sites certainly moved elsewhere, and their descendants are believed to be the residents of present-day pueblos and villages.

The essence of the Southwest is well distilled in Canyon de Chelly National Monument in northeastern Arizona. The twisting red-rock gorges, up to 1,000 feet deep, marked by a sparkling trail of water in the spring and after heavy rains, and glowing in the slanting rays of the late and early sun, meet just about everybody's definition of "canyon country." Canyon de Chelly and its major tributary, Canyon del Muerto, were long the home of the ancients, and evidence of several hundred prehistoric villages, including large cliff houses, have been found.

Tool marks at the base of a cliff at Chaco Canyon where tools were sharpened in the sandstone. The Chacoans had a well-organized and smoothly functioning society, probably dominated by religious leaders.

A portion of the ruin at Pueblo Bonito in Chaco Canyon. The Chacoans abandoned their towns late in the 12th century, apparently because of a long drought. Even their extensive irrigation system could not deliver enough water.

West Ruin in Aztec Ruins north of Chaco Canyon National Monument was built between A.D. 1106 and 1124. Construction is dated by examining the tree rings on the logs used in the building of this structure. This housing complex was built on ground overlooking the Animas River, whose bottomlands provided fertile ground for crops.

A winter view of Aztec Ruins near Farmington, New Mexico. This housing complex was built on ground overlooking the Animas River, whose bottomlands provided fertile ground for crops.

The Great Kiva at Aztec Ruins, the only reconstruction of one of these ceremonial chambers in North America. It is likely that members of the community gathered here for socializing.

Tyuonyi Ruin, Bandelier National Monument, New Mexico. In addition to this ruin in Frijoles Canyon, a narrow gorge above the Rio Grande, the ancients also left cliff dwellings along the canyon walls. They used tools of hard stone to gouge cave rooms out of the soft deposits of compressed volcanic ash.

After a prolonged drought before 1300 forced abandonment of these sites, the canyons remained empty until Navajos occupied them around 1700. They fought so often with the Spanish and the Pueblo Indians that the former attacked the Navajos and killed 115 of them in a bastion thereafter known as Massacre Cave. The American government removed the Navajos to a reservation in New Mexico in 1864, but the tribe was so miserable that they were allowed to return to the canyons four years later. They live there today, still tending sheep in some cases.

Dwellings, rock art, and other artifacts of past human habitation are included within the boundaries of no fewer than eleven other national parks and monuments in Arizona.

Prehistoric Indian life is massively documented in Utah, the state where the many tributaries of the Colorado River have carved intricate patterns of interconnecting canyons. The ancients utilized the flowing water and fertile bottomland in the canyons, and lived and stored grain in the many amphitheaters and smaller recesses in the rock walls. Here, as elsewhere, archaeologists have found a gradual flowering of culture over a span of centuries, then a rather abrupt departure around 1300 after a drought of more than two decades.

Golden Spike National Historic Site, in the Promontory Mountains of northern Utah, commemorates a major event in the forging of a transcontinental nation. By 1861 the eastern states were linked by 31,000 miles of track, but the western territories were still isolated. Congress authorized the construction of a railroad by the Central Pacific (from the west) and the Union Pacific (from the east). The termini were Sacramento, California and Omaha, Nebraska. The rails met at Promontory Point, in Utah, on May 10, 1869, after 1,776 miles of track were laid over deserts, rivers, and mountains while the workers occasionally fended off harassing Indians. Civil War veterans, unemployed immigrants, and former slaves, as well as 10,000 Chinese imported for the purpose, provided most of the hard labor required to accomplish this feat.

The Park System has 50 units officially designated as national parks, and only one of them was created primarily because of its cultural (rather than natural) resources. That is Mesa Verde in southwestern Colorado. In about A.D. 550 groups of Anasazi people chose to live on and below a level plateau heavily forested with pinyon and juniper trees and dissected with deep canyons leading down to a valley. Centuries later, the Spanish would call the plateau Mesa Verde ("green table").

Painted Cave, in Bandelier, accessible by a two-day round-trip hike of 20 miles. These are pictographs, or paintings, left by the residents of this canyon region between the 9th and 13th centuries.

Salinas National Monument in New Mexico contains some of the best surviving examples of 17th century Spanish missions. Abó, constructed in the 1620s, served the surrounding pueblo community. The mission had an organ and a trained choir.

The missions in the Salinas Valley, including Abó, succeeded for some years, but the Spanish antagonized the Apaches with their slave raids. In retribution, the Apaches attacked the missions and their pueblos. A drought made life worse, and the Spanish and the Pueblo residents left the valley in the 1670s.

The mission at Quarai in the Salinas Valley also dates from the early 1600s. The Spanish introduced a legal system that protected the Indians' civil and property rights.

The 200-foot-high Inscription Rock is the most dramatic feature of El Morro National Monument in New Mexico. This outcropping, on an early travel route, attracted prehistoric artists, and in more recent times many travelers have inscribed their names. The earliest legible writing is by Don Juan de Oñate, the Spanish governor, in 1605. Hundreds of inscriptions were added later.

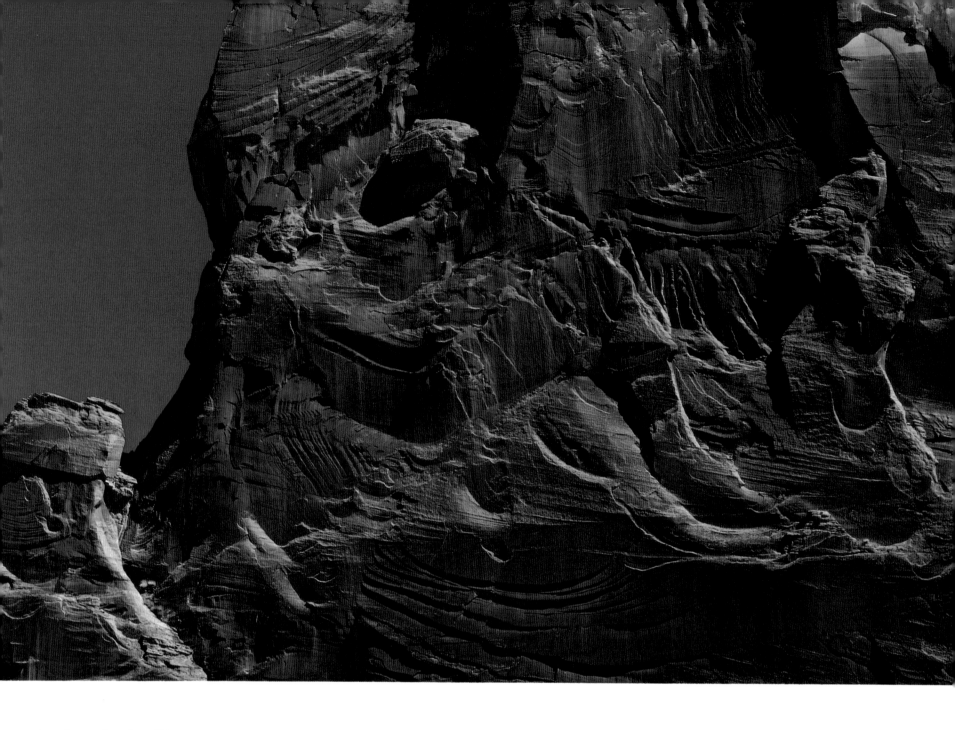

A sculptured rock wall in Canyon de Chelly. For thousands of years early Americans sought out these deep canyons because of the water that flows—occasionally, at least—through their convoluted passageways. Life can be harsh in the desert Southwest, but the scenery is mesmerizingly beautiful.

Petroglyphs, Petrified Forest National Park. Rock art is found in hundreds of places in the Southwest. The ancients usually etched their designs on a sheer cliff that had been covered with a deposit of desert varnish. This dark varnish consists of deposits of chemicals left on the wall after rainwater spilled down the surface.

The ruins of Fort Union, in New Mexico, that stand today are of the fort built in the mid-1860s. The largest military post in the Southwest, Fort Union closed after the railroad was completed to Santa Fe, providing a safe journey for travelers.

From 1851 to 1891 the fort protected settlers on the Santa Fe Trail. The earthworks at the bottom are from the fort that stood during the Civil War, when Confederates attacked. When Union forces destroyed the Southerners' supply train, the attackers withdrew, ending any Confederate attempt to seize the Southwest.

Montezuma Castle in central Arizona is a misnomer. Montezuma never got near the place. It is one of the best preserved of all ancient ruins, being 90 percent complete.

Hopi House, on the South Rim of the Grand Canyon. A registered historical landmark, it was constructed in 1905 and modeled after the Hopi Indian pueblo of Old Oraibi.

A stone pick axe from Montezuma Castle. The five-story, 20-room castle, well above the valley floor, was accessible only by ladders.

The largest cliff dwellings in Arizona are in Navajo National Monument. Navajos never lived there, but migrating members of the tribe discovered these 13th century structures. This is Betatakin, a village constructed in a large alcove within a canyon.

The Anasazi were a Stone Age people who were skillful at creating functional and lovely baskets and shaping bones, wood, and stone into a variety of tools. Later they learned the art of making pottery. Initially hunters and gatherers of wild plants, they turned more to the growing of crops. During their classic period, 1100 to 1300, they constructed some of the largest and most solidly built cliff dwellings in the world, tucked within the giant alcoves nature had so conveniently carved in cliff walls through the expedients of flash floods and other natural occurrences.

Then, about 1300, like their kinsmen elsewhere on the Colorado Plateau, the Anasazi moved on, perhaps in the face of that pervasive drought, and settled elsewhere. They left behind, in their pots and baskets, and in their trash piles, tantalizing clues to their world in a small corner of the vast and empty Southwestern desert.

Fort Laramie National Historic Site in Wyoming recalls more than five decades of frontier adventure. A trading post was established there in 1834, and the site became a major post until the fur trade subsided. Then Fort Laramie became a stopping point for emigrants bound for the Northwest on the Oregon Trail. As Indian harassment accelerated, it became a major outpost for forays against the Sioux warriors. The post declined in importance after hostilities subsided in the 1880s, and the fort was abandoned.

At Custer Battlefield National Monument in eastern Montana, history blurs with legend, heroism blends with foolhardiness, and the romance of war almost obscures its gore. The trail to the Little Bighorn River began at Fort Laramie in 1868, when the United States signed a treaty setting aside a large area as a reservation for the Sioux, Cheyenne, and other tribes. When gold was discovered in the Black Hills—within the reservation boundaries—thousands of whites swarmed in and the tribes revolted against the treaty.

A Navajo hogan, Navajo National Monument. This earthen structure was, until a few decades ago, the most common type of home for the Navajos, who live in northeastern Arizona and portions of adjacent states.

The Anasazi moved to Betatakin to establish new agriculture fields in Tsegi Canyon. The alcove village could have held about 125 people. By 1300, after only 50 years, it was abandoned, probably because arroyos cut deeply into the canyon floor, lowered the water table, and dried the soil.

The Franciscans began building Mission San José de Tumacacori in Arizona about 1800, but it was never completed. In 1821 Mexico gained its independence from Spain and funding dried up.

After the Indians refused to return to the reservation, the army moved in. At the Little Bighorn on June 25, 1876, General George Armstrong Custer, an ambitious and, some would say, rash commander, attacked a superior force of Sioux and Cheyenne. He and all others in five companies of the Seventh Cavalry, some 225 men in all, were wiped out on the grassy slopes above the quiet, meandering stream. Custer was dead, but the saga of his "last stand" lives on.

Though they had won at Little Bighorn, the Indians soon gave up their resistance and returned to the reservation. Another tragic episode in the conflict along the frontier ended a year later. The Nez Percé Indians were fleeing from their reservation, some 800 people in all including women and children, and 2,000 horses. They clashed repeatedly with the army during an epic journey through four states. At Big Hole National Battlefield, in western Montana, on August 9 and 10, 1877, the Nez Percé beat back a surprise attack and resumed their flight.

After a trek of 1,700 miles, and only 30 miles short of sanctuary in Canada, the Nez Percé finally gave up in October 1877. In one of the most poignant acknowledgements of defeat, their heroic leader, Chief Joseph, said:

"I am tired of fighting. Our chiefs are killed…. The little children are freezing to death. My people, some of them, have run away to the hills, and have no blankets, no food…. I want to have time to look for my children…Here me, my chiefs. I am tired; my heart is sick and sad. From where the sun now stands, I will fight no more forever."

The interior of Tumacacori. This mission served the Pima people. Mexico sold the land in 1844, and Apache raids forced the Indians to leave for another mission in 1848. They took the furnishings with them.

Hubbell Trading Post, on the Navajo Indian Reservation in Arizona, is filled with coffee, flour, sugar, blankets, tobacco, canned goods, and many other items. To obtain these products or credit, the Navajos would bring in their colorful handwoven rugs and beautiful turquoise and silver jewelry.

The trading post was founded by John Lorenzo Hubbell in 1876. It is still in business. The Hubbells brought the white man and the Indian together, by employing Navajos themselves and by finding jobs in white-owned businesses for others. Hubbell also hired a teacher for the Navajos.

Utah has one of the world's greatest concentrations of prehistoric rock art. These petroglyphs, etched into the canyon wall, are in Dinosaur National Monument. Efforts continue to interpret the meaning of the etchings. The antennae are especially curious.

The simple but graphic art of the early Americans make them seem like a real presence in the shadowed, mysterious canyons of the Colorado Plateau. This sheep petroglyph in Capitol Reef National Park could have been created yesterday. Drawings of sheep near game trails may have been intended to bring luck in the hunt.

Ruins of Hovenweep National Monument in Utah. Not all of the large structures were built within canyon alcoves. This complex was built here to protect springs. Access to water was, and is, the most critical factor relating to survival in the desert.

Brigham Young, president of the Mormon Church, directed that a fort be built at Pipe Spring to protect the water. A ranch was established to which the Mormon faithful donated cattle as their means of tithing. The herd generated profits for the church through the sale of cheese, butter, and beef.

Pipe Spring National Monument preserves a green oasis in the vast lonely section of desert called the Arizona Strip. The free-flowing spring had attracted Native Americans and other travelers for centuries.

A section of the Cliff Palace, the largest ruin in Mesa Verde National Park. At first the Anasazi lived in pit houses dug into the ground, but by A.D. 1100 they had begun building these apartment complexes in canyon alcoves. The Cliff Palace, built in the 1200s, contains more than 200 rooms. Religious activities probably took place in the circular kivas, or ceremonial rooms.

Spruce Tree Ruin, another prehistoric village at Mesa Verde. They were constructed largely of sandstone, cut into breadloaf-size blocks. The mortar was a mix of mud and water. Rooms were about six feet by eight feet, enough for two or three persons. Most daily work routine occurred in the courtyards in front of the rooms.

To the right is a portion of Mesa Verde ("green table") in southwestern Colorado. The tree-carpeted plateau, 15 by 20 miles, rises up to 2,000 feet above the valley floor. It was this place, 14 centuries ago, that the Anasazi chose to live. The soil provides opportunities for farming.

Bent's Old Fort, built in southeastern Colorado in 1833-34, was the hub of American influence in the region, a center for fur trading, and a way station on the Santa Fe Trail. Soldiers, settlers, and gold-seekers fouled the watering places, used up wood, and frightened away the bison. The owner abandoned the fort in 1849. This is a reconstruction.

Historic buildings in Old Trail Town, in Cody, Wyoming, reassembled on the site of the frontier town of Old Cody. The outlaw Butch Cassidy and the Sundance Kid hid out in one of the log cabins.

Fort Clatsop National Memorial, in Oregon, near the mouth of the Columbia River, includes a reconstruction of the fort built by the expedition of Meriwether Lewis and William Clark in 1805. The arrival of Lewis and Clark at the Pacific Ocean climaxed the westward half of one of history's most challenging overland expeditions.

The recorded history of California begins just 50 years after Columbus, in 1542—and before the dawn of history on the East Coast at St. Augustine, Fort Raleigh, and Jamestown. Juan Rodríguez Cabrillo was Portuguese-born, but his epic voyage of discovery was in the service of Spain. On September 28, 1542 he stepped ashore at a harbor we know today as San Diego, and claimed possession for Spain. The ship was met by a people "comely and large" who wore animal skins.

Continuing up the coast, Cabrillo's crew saw the valleys, plains, and mountains of California. Cabrillo fell and broke his leg, and it became infected. He died on January 3, 1543, while the ship was anchored off San Miguel Island, one of the Channel Islands. Cabrillo National Monument in San Diego honors this intrepid explorer.

Two units of the Park system are among the many attractions of San Francisco. Fort Point, a Civil War-era brick structure, guards the harbor at its narrow entrance. The Golden Gate National Recreation Area encompasses many natural and historic features, including ships of the National Maritime Museum, various military properties, and Alcatraz Island, site of the former prison.

Moulton Barn, in Jackson Hole, beneath the peaks of the Grand Tetons in Wyoming. The Park Service is buying old buildings like this one to preserve the rustic flavor of this beautiful part of the western frontier.

Fort Laramie saw a lot of Western history—as a center of the fur trade, as a way station and source of supplies for travelers on the Oregon Trail, as a stop on the Pony Express, and finally as a military base for the U.S. Army.

Interior of barracks, Fort Laramie. In the 1830s and 1840s, traders dealt amicably with the Sioux here, but tensions rose as more forts were built and more settlers came through. The army, often inept in its dealings with the Sioux, suffered several bloody defeats at their hands. Laramie was a logistical center during the campaign against the Sioux in 1876.

General George Armstrong Custer and all 225 men in his command died on June 25, 1876 above the Little Bighorn River in a fight against Sioux and Cheyenne. The stones in the foreground mark where soldiers fell. A national cemetery is in the distance.

Grant-Kohrs Ranch National Historic Site in Montana illustrates development of the Northern Plains cattle industry from the 1850s on. Activities introduce visitors to the heyday of the cowboy as well as modern ranching.

Nez Percé National Historical Park embraces 24 sites in central Idaho important to the history and culture of this tribe. Geological formations, historic buildings, and a trading post are among places of interest. This is White Bird Battlefield, where the Nez Percé, fleeing from the army in 1877, defeated the soldiers and killed 34 of them while suffering no deaths.

The bastion at the reconstructed Fort Vancouver, a national historic site in Washington. From 1825 to 1849, the fort was the western headquarters of the Hudson's Bay Company fur trading operations. The fort, on the Columbia River, was in British territory until an 1846 treaty assigned it to the United States.

Lava Beds National Monument, near the Oregon border, contains an inhospitable landscape of hardened volcanic lava in myriad grotesque forms. It was here in 1872 and 1873 that the Modoc Indians, unwilling to submit to life on a reservation, fought bravely and—for a time—victoriously against an army up to 20 times their number before giving up.

Death Valley, protected in a national monument primarily because of its stark, otherworldly scenery, has seen human history, too. Emigrants unlucky enough to get lost there gave the valley its name in 1849, though they in fact didn't die there. The discovery of borax and the need to transport the ore gave rise to the famous 20-mule teams.

Historic sites and parks in Hawaii include the ruins of the temple built by King Kamehameha the Great, the so-called City of Refuge where lawbreakers and vanquished warriors could escape death by reaching sacred ground, and the site of an isolated colony where lepers were sent—often described as a living tomb. Today much progress has been made in treating leprosy, and victims of this disease are no longer excluded from contact with other human beings.

Marcus and Narcissa Whitman established a Protestant mission at this site, Waiilatpu ("place of rye grass") in Washington in 1836. The mission was a stopping point on the Oregon Trail. A measles epidemic in 1847 killed half of the Cayuse tribe. The survivors, angered by this disease caught from whites, attacked the mission and killed the Whitmans and others.

The National Maritime Museum in San Francisco includes a floating museum of five ships. The island, Alcatraz, also a part of Golden Gate National Recreation Area, was once a maximum security Federal penitentiary. Called "The Rock" by its inmates, the prison housed such criminals as Al Capone, Machine Gun Kelly, and Robert Stroud, the "Birdman of Alcatraz."

Fort Point, now in the shadow of the Golden Gate Bridge, was built by the Army Corps of Engineers at the entrance to San Francisco harbor between 1853 and 1861. Designed to mount 126 muzzle-loading cannon and house 500 soldiers under wartime conditions, the garrison never fired a shot in anger.

Bodie, a state park, is well past its prime. But in 1879, during the height of the gold rush on the high desert east of the Sierra Nevada, it claimed 10,000 residents. Bodie was a violent town even by frontier standards, with killings occurring about once a day.

Scotty's Castle, built in Death Valley in the 1920s, was the vacation retreat for a wealthy Chicagoan, Albert Johnson. His friend and frequent guest, Walter Scott, had proposed this remote location for this extravagant dwelling, and it was informally named after him.

After the Johnsons and Scott died, the Federal government purchased the ranch. The "castle" contains lovely furnishings and art objects.

Pu'uhonua o Honaunau (formerly City of Refuge) National Historical Park on the island of Hawaii. Warriors vanquished in battle and violators of the sacred laws, or kapu, could find sanctuary in this refuge. After staying there a day, the refugee returned home and all was forgiven. Until kapu was abolished, laws were severe: death was the penalty for someone whose shadow fell on the palace grounds.

This temple was built by Kamehameha the Great in 1790-1791 on the island of Hawaii. He dedicated it to his war god to bring good fortune in battle. He then invited his rival to a peace parley. The rival was killed and sacrificed at the temple to the god.

The USS Utah *Memorial at Pearl Harbor. This training ship capsized on being struck by the Japanese. In addition to the Arizona, three other ships were sunk, and three more were damaged. Japanese attacks killed 2,403 U.S. soldiers and civilians and wounded 1,178.*

This aerial photograph was taken by a Japanese pilot from an attacking plane at Pearl Harbor on December 7, 1941. The planes struck at about 7:55 on a Sunday morning. The attack was a surprise; an earlier U.S. radar report of approaching planes was not treated seriously.

The USS Arizona *Memorial. Struck by a 1,760-pound bomb during the Japanese attack, the Arizona exploded and then sank within nine minutes. It still lies beneath this shrine, the tomb for some 1,000 of her crew.*

The men buried on the Arizona are named on this honor roll within the memorial. The white concrete and steel memorial building spans the 186-foot hull of the sunken ship.

American Memorial Park on Saipan in the Mariana Islands in the Pacific, the scene of bitter fighting during World War II. These weapons are at the last Japanese command post.

The National Memorial Cemetery of the Pacific on Punchbowl Hill in Honolulu contains the graves of more than 13,000 killed in World War II and the Korean War.

141

Sitka National Historical Park, site of the last serious stand by the Tlingit Indians against Russian colonization. The tribe successfully defended a wooden fort here in 1804 for six days, but withdrew because of a lack of ammunition. Totem poles are an impressive cultural achievement of the Tlingits.

Off the Hawaiian island of Oahu, the USS *Arizona* Memorial marks the spot where the battleship was sunk on December 7, 1941, during the Japanese attack on Pearl Harbor.

Alaska is the most sparsely populated state of the Union, and yet, as long as the United States has had a human history it has had one in Alaska.

Two units of the Park System recall events of quite recent times. Sitka National Historical Park is the site of the Tlingit Indian fort and a battle in 1804 that marked the last major resistance to Russian colonization. Klondike Gold Rush National Historical Park preserves historic buildings that stood during the 1898 gold rush.

In the far northwest of Alaska, above the Arctic Circle and along the shore of the Chukchi Sea, a remarkable archaeological record is spread across the gravels. Here, at Cape Krusenstern National Monument, Eskimo people have hunted marine mammals for 4,000 years. Within 114 lateral beach ridges, reading chronologically from the inland to the water, lie artifacts, including tools and weapons, from every known Eskimo occupation of North America.

To the southwest, just below the Arctic Circle, at the westernmost extension of the North American mainland, some 2.78 million acres have been set aside as Bering Land Bridge National Preserve. This is where it all began. During the glacial epoch 14,000 to 25,000 years ago, a land bridge joined America and Asia. Across this bridge, it appears likely, came the prehistoric hunters who were the ancestors of all the Native peoples of the Western Hemisphere.

Those who trekked from Siberia and lands further away began the process of peopling the United States. The first Americans came in search of big game and a better environment for living. They and the Europeans, Africans, and other Asians who came later have made quite a history. Today that history continues to unfold, as Americans continue to search and strive.

Modern Skagway, population about 1,000. In 1897-1898, Skagway grew from one cabin to a population of 15,000. Many historic buildings have been preserved in the National Historical Park.

INDEX BY PAGE

INDEX BY PHOTOGRAPHER

The Publishers would like to thank the National Park Service for their kind assistance with this project. Special thanks go to Cathy Chase, Rosa Wilson, James C. Roach, Jim Voigt, Sue Pridemore, Rich Tourangeau and Tom Durant.